The Temple of Antoninus and Faustina in the Roman Forum
encloses the Church of St. Lawrence in Miranda

LEFT
Pulpit, St. Lawrence-
Outside-the-Walls

LEFT, BELOW
St. John Bosco and
St. Pius X lie in
state outside
St. Peter's

RIGHT
A Swiss Guard recruit
takes the oath of
fidelity to the Pope

RIGHT, BELOW
Mosaic facade,
St. Paul's Outside-
the-Walls

Bernini colonnade, plaza of St. Peter's

THIS IS ROME

THIS IS
ROME

A PILGRIMAGE
IN WORDS AND PICTURES

CONDUCTED BY FULTON J. SHEEN

PHOTOGRAPHED BY YOUSUF KARSH

DESCRIBED BY H. V. MORTON

WITH AN INTRODUCTION BY

BISHOP SHEEN

HAWTHORN BOOKS, INC.

PUBLISHERS · NEW YORK

First Edition, March 1960

The Scripture translations throughout are from *The Holy Bible,* translated by Ronald Knox, Copyright 1944, 1948, 1950, Sheed and Ward, Inc., New York.

Nihil Obstat

JOSEPH H. BRADY, s.t.d.
CENSOR LIBRORUM

Imprimatur

THOMAS A. BOLAND, s.t.d.
ARCHBISHOP OF NEWARK

January, 1960

CONTENTS

INTRODUCTION

TO SEE Rome through the eyes of a boy has certain advantages and certain disadvantages. The advantage is that a boy sees it through a telescope, while an adult sees it through a microscope. Youth sees it big through the small end; age sees its tiny details from the big end. What tremendous fascination there is for a boy to see St. Peter's through a keyhole, as one of the photographs in this book shows him doing. Perhaps there is no better way of seeing a church built to honor a man to whom were given the keys of the Kingdom of Heaven, than to see it through a door. In a few years, when the boy grows older, he may recall seeing the ruins of the Forum of Julius Caesar, but for the moment his mind has a different association: "Oh, that is where all the cats were." Seeing Julius Caesar through cats is not so different from thinking of Aunt Harriet in terms of sugar cookies. To some extent great geniuses perceive the mighty through the trivial as Wordsworth did once when walking through the forests: "Down on your knees, man; thank God there are violets." And once upon a time a mother looked down on a Babe in her arms and saw Heaven.

But there also can be a disadvantage in seeing Rome through the eyes of a boy; he is apt to think the dead are dead, and that Rome is very ancient.

To me, Rome seemed very young, because monuments, catacombs, and obelisks were palpitating with meaning and life. Parents seem very old to children, but when the children have families of their own, they discover that the ideas they once called "old-fashioned" are fresh with novelty. Rome is full of tombs to one who is not yet ten; but when he grows older, he will hear voices coming from these tombs, and will realize that the wisdom and proverbs of a Gregory or a Leo XIII are repeated, not because they are proverbial, but because they are practical and timeless. Because youth often sees the past as dead, he is sometimes in revolt against the present. But maturity sees that that which is called modern is only a new name for something that is very ancient.

When anyone has what he thinks is a new, original idea, he ought to go back to see how Aristotle put it. The child who looks at the tomb of Dante, and sees written there the date of his birth and death, does not know how alive Dante is to the mind refreshed by his flaming thoughts. So the tomb of Peter may seem like a tomb to the young, but to those whom years and faith have ripened, Peter is walking in Rome, not as a ghost, but as a man in white.

This is Rome is the story of how Jerry Cunningham, our grandnephew, saw the Eternal City. To enable you to share that visit, only two things were necessary: a pen and a camera. The pen was held by H. V. Morton, who has reverently and sympathetically illumined more minds about the beauties of travel than anyone in our generation. The camera was needed too, not as something automatic to be clicked, but as an instrument to be used as a painter uses a brush. To Yousuf Karsh was entrusted the artistry of tracing figures and statues, dancing lights and fleeting shadows in photographs.

On the way to Rome we told Jerry how much that city was entwined with the life of Our Lord and the Apostles.

10

Model of ancient Rome, Foro Italico

It was Caesar Augustus, master bookkeeper of the world, seated at his desk by the Tiber, who unwittingly fulfilled the prophecy of Micheas that Christ would be born in Bethlehem. In obedience to his decree, Mary, who was of royal blood, went to David's town for the birth of Christ, the Son of God. The political ruler to whom the Child was first subject was Herod the Great, the representative of Roman world authority in that area.

During His Public Life, the uppermost question for the conquered people among whom Our Lord moved was: "Is it lawful to pay tribute to Caesar?" The Son of God made Man, answering, implied that He had other ways of dealing with Rome. He would leave Caesar on his throne, Roman procurators in their multiplied palaces, Caesar's legions on their streets and Roman coinage in their pockets: "Render to Caesar the things that are Caesar's and to God the things that are God's."

11

He would deal with Rome in His own divine way.

Although praising a Roman centurion for his faith, He avoided all political entanglements with Rome, even when Satan claimed the world as his own and boasted of the power to deliver it to anyone he pleased. The first suggestion of the role Rome was to play in the plans of His Kingdom was revealed in the two cities wherein Christ communicated to Peter his double role in the Church: first, that of exercising the power of keys with the promised security against the gates of hell; and second, the authority to rule and govern the flock committed to his care.

One of the cities was Caesarea Philippi, in which was a grotto to the pagan god, Pan. In a place named after Caesar and a fawning Roman procurator, Our Lord gave to Peter the power of keys saying that upon him, the Rock, "I will build My Church." The other city was Tiberias, named after the then reigning Roman emperor. Christ there gave to Peter the order to rule and govern His Church under the symbol of feeding His lambs and sheep. He Who called Himself the Good Shepherd now confers His shepherding powers on the Man called Peter.

In cities named after the Caesars, the Lord of History would dethrone Caesar, not the Caesar who was a political ruler, but the Caesar who claimed to unify all men. In those outposts of Rome named after Romans who claimed to be pontiffs, He named a new Pontiff; in those very towns which represented the sovereignty of the Caesars, He created a new sovereignty, based not on armies of screaming legions, but on Divine authority communicated only after Peter had three times pledged his love of the Divine Master. Rome would indeed remain the center of the world's unity and all roads would continue to lead to Rome; but the dynasty of a Caesar who made himself a god would give place to the dynasty of a Peter who called himself the servant of the servants of God.

Peter went to Rome. When the persecution of Nero against the Christians broke out, tradition has it, Peter fled from Rome. Two miles down the Appian Way, on the very spot where today stands

St. Peter,
steps of
St. Peter's

13

the little church of Domine, Quo Vadis, Peter saw a vision of Christ returning to Rome bearing His Cross. "Whither goest Thou, Lord?" he asked in amazement. "I go to *Rome*," He said, "to be crucified again." Peter then said, "Lord, I return to be crucified with Thee."

Not long before the Lord told Peter, "I go to Rome," Paul, a former bigot and persecutor of Christians, who had become a convert, said, "I must see Rome." The root of this desire was in his association with Priscilla and Aquila,who had come straight from Rome to tell Paul of the devout Christians there, and of the perpetual influx of strangers from all of the world.

Finally, one day, almost at the end of his life, he came down those immortal stones of the Appian Way lined on both sides with the tombs of the dead, to bring the message of eternal life and the Resurrection. His heart leaped with joy as he saw the glittering marble dancing in the sunlight. "This is Rome." For at last he saw it, but he saw it as a prisoner chained to a soldier. Some nearsighted men bemoaned the fact that Paul's good works were cut short because of his being shut in the Mamertine prison, but Paul wrote, "I hasten to assure you that my circumstances have had only the effect of spreading the Gospel further; so widely has my imprisonment contributed to the Gospel."

Peter and Paul both met their death in Rome; Peter through a crucifixion, as Our Lord foretold, and Paul through the sword. Fittingly, the man called the Rock was crucified, at his own request, head downward; for where else but in the earth should the foundation rock of the Church be laid? Paul, who so often spoke of the sword of the Spirit, lost his head through the sword of a Nero.

According to an ancient legend the founders of pagan Rome were Romulus and Remus, two brothers who were nourished on the non-human food of a wolf. As we looked at that statue on the Capitoline Hill, our mind flashed to the two founders of Christian Rome, Peter and Paul, who were nourished by the nonhuman Bread of the God Man.

St. Paul,
steps of
St. Peter's

In any case, there are two Romes to see—the Rome that boasted of its eternity because of the might of the army whose eagles screamed victoriously over the world; the other, the Christian Rome in which waters from a thousand fountains seem to fall upward as well as downward as they gush from an underground sea, and which became an Eternal City because a Fisherman came to live there.

H. V. Morton tells, in the pages to follow, the story of what Jerry saw in Rome. But there are different reflections we would add to those already described: one, about underground Rome; the other, about the effect the trip will have on the boy in the years to come.

Men like excavations; hardly a man exists who has not stopped to see a steam-shovel dig a hole in the ground. But boys love caves, probably because they are mysterious. Caves are like ancient libraries containing the wisdom of the centuries. Some caves contain a record of man, his arts, his tools, his drawings, however crude. Bethlehem, for example, had a cave wherein was born the Divinity Who shook the earth to its very foundations.

The underground caves of Rome hold fascination for any youth.

Wolf suckling
Romulus and Remus,
Capitoline Hill

16

The catacombs alone, according to the estimate of Giovanni Battista de Rossi, have an aggregate gallery length of 587 miles. On both sides of the corridors, which often are four stories deep, are niches in which the dead were buried. In the catacombs of St. Callistus is the Chapel of the Popes, so called because in it are buried some of the early Popes* who died martyrs: St. Zephyrinus (119-217), St. Pontian (230-235), St. Anteros (who reigned only two months, 235-6, and was martyred by Maximian), St. Fabian (236-250), and others. The inscriptions are in Greek, the language of the Gospels and Epistles as well as the proceedings of the first twelve Councils of the Church. St. Callistus who was the Pope (217-222) after whom the catacomb was named, actually is not buried there; he was martyred by being thrown from a window, his remains being found in the Catacomb of Calepodius.

Jerry served our Mass in that Chapel of the Popes. There under the floor of the great city we telescoped the Last Supper and the Mass; but we also united in our faith John XXIII and his predecessors who lived within 150 years of St. Peter. The very garments we wore at Mass differed but little from the togas worn by Horace or Catullus or the man of the street in Rome of the third century; and the Creed which Jerry and we recited did not differ from the Creed of the Popes buried round about us as the Abrahams, Isaacs and Jacobs of the New Law, now gathered to the Father in Heaven. Here there was more than a sequence of historical events; there was rather an unbroken succession of life, truth and love.

In those same cavernous depths was another confirmation of the Psalmist: "Though a hundred trials beset the innocent, the Lord will bring him safely through them all. Under the Lord's keeping, every bone of his is safe." For there too was the tomb of the beautiful St. Cecilia who was martyred in 224. In 820 Pope Paschal I had seen

* *Note:* The Annuario Pontificio 1959 gives different dates for these Popes. This is the semi-official Vatican Directory and its list of Popes was prepared by an expert: St. Pontian (230-235); St. Anteros (Nov. 21, 235—Jan. 3, 236); St. Fabian (Jan. 10, 236—Jan. 20, 250).

in a dream her body's resting place in this catacomb "fresh and perfect as when it was first laid in the tomb, with linen cloths stained with blood rolled up at her feet." The hidden resting place was discovered and a sculptor made a replica of the maid as found, seemingly asleep, the mark of the sword on her neck, and with three fingers outstretched expressing in death that which her life confessed: a belief in the Three Persons of the Blessed Trinity.

Jerry wanted to know if there were not really more martyrs today under Communism than there were under the Roman emperors. We assured Jerry that there probably were, and that is why he may expect a more glorious world when Communism falls just as the Christians of those days evangelized the world after Rome fell.

Plato said that all knowledge is a recall from another world, and that we remember ideas from a previous existence. This theory is untrue, because all our knowledge begins with the senses. But one who visits Rome, as this boy did, will later on, as he studies, have the impression that he is recalling the events of a previous experience. The pages of a history book will not be opaque to him, like a curtain, but transparent, like a window pane.

Who is there who has ever studied Cicero, Virgil, Horace, or Tacitus and does not wish that these characters were more than assignments for credits? To have seen the spot where a noble Caesar fell, by a deed second in infamy only to that of Judas Iscariot; to have trod the land of Horace's Sabine farm, the most famous farm in literature, "that corner of the earth that smiled before all others"; to have been in the city that Virgil prophesied has "no fixed goal to achievement, no end to empire . . . authority without limit"; to have walked over the ruins of the Palatine wherein stood the palace of Augustus, and in front of which he used to beg alms from passers-by once a year, to remind himself to be frugal—such sightseeing makes these names vibrate with flesh and blood. And even though there come moments in the life of every Latin student when he wishes

18

Virgil had stuck to his threat to throw his *Aeneid* into the fire, there will nevertheless be a moral lesson of stick-to-it-tive-ness in the fact that Virgil spent eleven years polishing and perfecting that poem.

To a youth, ancient Rome may seem at first a town of tombs, but the more he dips into the wisdom of the ages, the more he will discover that each tomb has its resurrection, as mortality puts on immortality. No mind is stamped with the sinister bar of illegitimacy if it can point to its origins. Because Rome is terribly alive, the monuments of the Pope are not like the kings of France in the Cathedral of St. Denis stretched out flat; rather they are flamboyant, moving either like orators on fire or judges with accusing fingers—— marble though they be, they seem not dead, but alive.

The climax of our trip was our visit with His Holiness, Pope John XXIII. *Ubi Petrus, ibi ecclesia*——"where Peter is, there is the Church." In a short time the world has come to love this heir to Peter. On a plane, not long ago, I found a delightful traveling companion in a Greek Orthodox bishop who, in the course of conversation, brought up the subject of Pope John XXIII. "No words of mine," he said, "can express my sentiments better than the Fourth Gospel," which he quoted in Greek. "A man appeared, sent from God, whose name was John."

A man of God with a common name on an uncommon mission— such was the description of the Pontiff in the cameo of that tiny text.

Pope John XXIII has three dimensions: First, *depth*, inasmuch as he is rooted to the soil, to the peasantry, to the earth, to the common people. The Lord Whom he represents called Himself the "Son of Man" over fifty-five times to indicate His oneness with humanity. That fellowship with mankind, symbolized by the most common of names, John, and then made more common still by raising it to the twenty-third power, reveals him, not only as the world's Holy Father, but also the world's Holy Brother.

Breadth is the second dimension of his character. One of his first appointments as a priest was to be National Director of the Society for the Propagation of the Faith in Italy. The poor, the ignorant, the sick, the distressed of Asia, Africa, and Oceania were thrust into his hands for sympathetic understanding. But in a century of world wars, who could claim to embrace all classes of men without being a chaplain to soldiers? The young priest became a chaplain. Then, that he might understand as Pontiff the woes and wounds of those imprisoned behind the Iron Curtain, Providence missioned him to Bulgaria. That the expansiveness of a heart might not be fenced in by the memory of ancient historical quarrels, but rather enlarged to embrace all who might later want to sit in Council with him, he came to know first hand, among others, Moslems and Orthodox in Turkey and Greece. The symbol of charity is not the circle circumscribed by self, but the Cross with arms outstretched to embrace all humanity within its grasp. This symbol worn on the breast of Pope John XXIII is merely the reflection of the love of mankind in his heart.

Finally, there is the dimension of *height*. Love of humanity without love of the Heavenly Father would mean we were all a race of illegitimate children. For him the other two dimensions flow from his piety or his relation to God. As he was so fond of saying: "Always respect the dignity of those you are with, and above all, the freedom of every human being. God Himself does."

No one better recognizes than a Supreme Pontiff that his power comes from God, in virtue of his office; but virtue or holiness, he also knows, must come from himself through prayer and sacrifice. The combination of trust in God and his open humility manifested itself throughout the audience with him.

When speaking to Jerry, His Holiness told him about all the saints who were named Jerome and the character of each. From saints, the Holy Father passed to the subject of the priesthood, saying to Jerry: "I hope some day God may call you to be a priest."

That would make not only the Holy Father happy—but also the uncle of Jerry.

MOST REVEREND FULTON J. SHEEN, D.D., PH.D.

I

THE ROME OF
THE CAESARS

THE VIA APPIA

UPON a recent morning in May two figures stood upon the Via Appia near Rome. One was a Bishop in clerical hat and cassock; the other a boy of about nine years of age. Those who happened to be passing along the Appian Way at that moment, for the old road is still lively, must have thought them a pleasing contrast: age and youth; experience and innocence; priest and catachumen; and some may even have been aware that in that particular spot, and under a Roman sky, they achieved a deeper symbolism—a Bishop pointing out the way to a young Christian.

Their presence upon the Queen of Roads[1] is simply explained. The Bishop had come to Rome upon the business of the Church and had brought his young grandnephew with him to show him the monuments and the shrines, for the boy was at the most receptive of ages and was also interested in such things. This glimpse of the Via Appia was the young pilgrim's introduction to the Eternal City.

What an interesting starting point, and one that could have been selected only by someone who had lived and studied in Rome; for here, before the mind becomes confused with temples, churches and

---

[1] *Appia longarum teritur regina viarum*—Statius, Sylv. II. 2. 12.

23

shrines, and the names and dates of emperors, Popes, and saints, is something simple and memorable for the imagination to seize upon: an old road going on to Rome in one direction and, in the other, to the south. Between the ruins of the tombs that line the Via Appia the land falls away here and there, giving a view of Rome herself, some miles off, enthroned upon her Seven Hills.

Julius Caesar, who for a time was responsible for the Appian Way and spent a great deal of his own money in repairing it, would be astonished could he stand today upon the old road and look at Rome. Perhaps he would not even recognize it. In his day it was a city of columns and temples; now it is a city of domes and churches. It may be, however, that there is still something in the lie of the land; in the relationship of the Palatine to the Caelian and the Aventine hills, in the position of the Janiculum across the Tiber, that would help a man from imperial times to recognize it with some difficulty, and certainly with amazement, as Rome.

Like many of the great military roads that covered the Roman Empire, the Via Appia carries down the centuries the name of its creator, Appius Claudius the Blind. He was the most powerful man in Rome in the year 312 B.C., the year he began the road which others eventually extended until it met the glitter of the Adriatic at Brundusium, which is now Brindisi. In his old age Appius Claudius became blind and retired from public life. But one day in the year 280 B.C. he was led into the Senate to make his last, and greatest, appearance. Pyrrhus, with whom Rome was at war, had gained a costly victory by flinging an elephant corps into the battle with much the same effect upon the Romans as the tanks had upon the Germans in the first World War. But the victory was merely technical and has given the word "Pyrrhic" to such achievements ever since. Maybe the startled Senate might have accepted the proffered peace terms had not Appius Claudius groped his way to his old seat in the assembly and given one of those demonstrations of the triumph of mind over matter, of spirit over physical frailty, which is confined

24

to no century and to no nation. He delivered a speech so courageous and so eloquent that the envoys returned to Pyrrhus with the message that Rome did not consider herself defeated. The speech has now been lost, but it was known and quoted in the time of Cicero. Such was the man who planned the Appian Way.

As the traveller approached Rome in ancient times, not only along the Via Appia but also upon all the main highways, he entered a city of the dead. Tombs rose on every side; consequently, before he had arrived, he was met everywhere by disconcerting gestures of farewell. His words of welcome were "good-bye for ever"—that pathetic pagan *Vale*—uttered by a thousand statues and tombstones, so that he proceeded upon his way to Rome, no doubt with chastened spirits, through a colossal marmoreal exhibition of family piety and grief that must have borne a strong resemblance to the main avenues of any *Campo Santo* in modern Italy.

The reason for this was the Roman law, inscribed upon the Twelve Tables, that no burial, even of ashes, might take place within the walls of a city. That is why the great cemeteries of Rome are to be found two or three miles away, along the lines of the main roads. It is also why St. Peter was buried in a cemetery on the Via Cornelia, which crossed the Vatican Hill, in a grave which now lies beneath the high altar of St. Peter's, and why St. Paul was buried in a suburban vineyard on the road to Ostia, in a grave that now lies beneath the high altar of St. Paul's-Outside-the-Walls. It is also the reason why the catacombs are all grouped round Rome at a distance of two or three miles.

All tombs were sacred under the Roman law, no matter what religion the dead may have practiced, and one of the most detestable of Roman crimes was *violatio sepulcri*, or the disturbance of human remains. It was the law that "every person makes the place that belongs to him a religious place at his own election by the carrying of his dead into it." It was also a recognized practice that executed persons should be handed over to relatives for burial, and that is why St. Joseph of Arimathea had no hesitation in asking Pilate for the body of Our Lord, and also why, even in times of persecution, bodies of the martyrs were so often given Christian burial. The bodies of St. Peter and St. Paul were at once claimed by their friends and buried. Only in times of the most furious persecutions in later centuries were these ancient principles disregarded.

The early Church inherited from the pagan world the horror of *violatio sepulcri,* and the thought that a martyr's bones might be disturbed was as abhorrent to the early Popes as to the Caesars. The letters of St. Gregory the Great are full of stern admonitions to those of the Eastern Church who asked him for relics, for such, as he explained, was not the practice of the Holy See. That great Pope would have been shocked to the depths of his being could he have known that the time would come when, after the barbarians had sacked the tombs and the catacombs in search of gold, the Church, in order to save the bones of the martyrs from destruction, brought them, often by the cartload, within the walls of Rome. So the custom of burial within the walls was forced upon the Church by invasion and disaster and thus became a Christian practice. No one living today could possibly imagine the dismay which such a thing would have inspired in the minds of a pagan Roman or an early Christian.

Such reflections, which are important to a proper understanding of Christian Rome, come naturally upon the Via Appia as one walks between lines of ancient tombs and, gazing across the countryside, sees the sunlight glinting upon a hundred Roman domes, each one rising above a church that contains the bones of a martyr. The re-entry of the dead Christians into Rome in the eighth century was not only a remarkable event in the world's history, but it also marked a change in thought which the primitive Church would have found difficult to accept.

Standing today upon the famous road, one realizes that it has altered considerably in the last hundred and fifty years. A great deal of the nineteenth century atmosphere has vanished with a good mo-

Original paving stones, Appian Way

toring surface: the solitude, the wind blowing over the malarial Campagna, the huge white oxen grazing by the wayside, the goatherd seated upon a fallen plinth, which we read about, and see in those delightful water-color sketches which our ancestors produced as easily as we take snapshots, have all more or less departed. The road that knew the firm tramp of the hobnailed legionaries now knows the rubbery shudder of a Vespa; and it is amusing to note how respectfully the motorist approaches those stretches of the original polygonal blocks of basalt that still exist. The Via Appia could probably not do much damage to a chariot, but it could easily wreck the back axle of a Fiat!

The sight of a Roman driving along the Via Appia on his Vespa, with his girl seated sideways behind him, is typical of that incongruous association of past and present, of heroic names of other times with the commonplace of today which is characteristic of Rome. It seems right and proper that a good bus service should link the Colosseum with the tomb of Caecilia Metella; and no Roman thinks it at all peculiar that upon the road where conquerors once led their legions home now stand country houses and villas whose owners often give cocktail parties to their neighbors on the Appian Way. Time, we are told, never stands still, but in Rome it has a tendency to hang about in curious pockets which appear motionless, such as the Franciscans in their monastery on the Via Appia above the Catacomb of St. Sebastian, who are just as Byron and Nathaniel Hawthorne saw them. They move about under the stone pines, and dig their garden, just as their predecessors did, and may be seen—odd sight in these days of cheap flashlights—grasping tapers wound round a stick as they lead tourists into the chilly depths.

Within a few yards of such changeless scenes the inquisitive or hungry stranger may discover, concealed behind a high wall covered with enormous white roses, a fashionable little restaurant. That the surprised visitor may see at the same moment a *maître d'hotel* and the tomb of Caecilia Metella, may appear incongruous, but it is not really so. The association of tombs and restaurants is a most ancient one, and gave St. Paul a good deal of trouble in Corinth.

One of the specialities of the restaurant on the Via Appia is grilled chicken which is wheeled ceremoniously to the table, drenched in cognac and then fired with boughs of laurel. There is something sacrificial and pagan about this dish in such a place, and at the crucial moment of combustion, as the dry laurel bursts into a tremendous crackling flame, it seems that the waiter's garments should suddenly be transformed into the toga of an officiating augur! It was probably H. G. Wells who wrote a short story about a man who passed through a gate in a very ordinary-looking wall and found himself in the Garden of the Hesperides, and it is with something of the same bewilderment, as if the time-machine had blown a fuse, that one concludes a meal upon the Appian Way. "Come, friend, and bring a flask of wine, together with the necessities for a potation," reads an ancient pagan epitaph, and Lanciani says, writing of ancient burials, "the Via Appia, the most popular cemetery in the suburbs of Rome, boasted of quite a large number of these *osterie della campagna*, where funeral banquets and potations could be ordered by relatives and friends of the departed ones."[2] How typical it is of the tenacity of Roman tradition that though the tombs should have fallen into ruin the grilled chicken is as good as ever!

The tradition of tomb feasts is indeed tenacious. Lanciani mentions a tavern which in his time stood outside the modern Roman cemetery of San Lorenzo all' Agro Verano called *Osteria dell' Anime Sante del Purgatorio*—"the Inn of the Blessed Souls in Purgatory."

Some six miles from Rome the Appian Way achieves something of its old atmosphere, and particularly in the evening, or under a gray sky, the funereal cypresses stand beside the road like monks with tapers. The wind, passing across the open spaces, comes sighing down the old highway; and it is then one remembers some of the

[2] Rodolfo Lanciani: *Wanderings through Ancient Roman Churches*

tragic events of this road. Here it was, one night in the year A.D. 65, that Seneca was resting in a villa on his way back to Rome from the country. A tribune knocked at the door and delivered to the philosopher the command of Nero that he should commit suicide for complicity in the Piso conspiracy, with which it is practically certain he had nothing to do. Some believe that Seneca was a Christian and a convert of St. Paul, but, however that may be, he was the good influence in Nero's boyhood. He was Nero's tutor and he was unable to flatter his pupil or to pretend that he was a great poet or a brilliant actor or singer, and gradually, as supreme power and flattery corroded the Emperor's character, he began to loathe where he had once loved. Seneca had also made the mistake of amassing a great fortune. Their relationship had some resemblance to that between Cardinal Wolsey and Henry VIII.

Upon receiving the death sentence, the Stoic calmly begged his friends not to grieve and ordered a doctor to open his veins. His young wife, Pompeia Paulina, insisted that she should die with him and, in a painful and distressing scene preserved by Tacitus, Seneca died; though Paulina's wrists were bound up at the Emperor's command and she was reluctantly snatched from death. Three years later, Nero himself, a terrified and hunted man, fled to the house of a freedman named Phaon upon the Appian Way. Suddenly finding himself deserted in the house, the Emperor realized that his hour had struck at last. As he remained hidden, he heard the sound of his pursuers upon the Appian Way and with last-minute courage he snatched up a sword and stabbed himself. The centurion who rushed into the room attempted to bind his wound. "It is too late," said Nero. "Is this your fidelity?"

Upon a sunny day with the wild flowers in the wayside grass and the poppies dotting the Campagna one comes along the Appian Way to an exquisite view of the Alban Hills, rising blue against the paler blue of the sky, their slopes covered with white towns that ascend even to the summits. The old road crosses them on its way to the south, and as one sees it one thinks of all those wayfarers

30

who in the course of twenty-two centuries have passed along it: Caesars and proconsuls with their courts and escorts; governors returning with the spoils of distant provinces; legions marching to attention as they passed each other, some on the way home to Rome, others bound for distant places on the frontiers of the world; Greek artists and writers seeking their fortune in the world's capital; caravans of wild animals with barbaric escorts, a cage of lions or a tank of crocodiles bound for the amphitheater; poets; jugglers; merchants; priests of Isis and Attis escorting their gods with drums and tambourines; and all moving along the *Regina Viarum* towards the Queen of Cities. How awed the peasants and the herdsmen must have been the day they watched the dead body of Sulla, who had died at Puteoli, come over the Appian Way "in a gilt litter, with royal ornaments, trumpets before him and horsemen behind," and again, at the sound of mournful horns, they must have gathered at the roadside to watch the great Augustus, who had expired at Nola in A.D. 14, pass onward to his palace on the Palatine, surrounded by those who believed that an age had ended, as indeed it had.

But greater than kings, and the greatest of the conquerors, were two who traveled to Rome upon the Appian Way, one a fisherman from Galilee, the other a tentmaker from Tarsus. When St. Peter and St. Paul came to Rome they brought Christ with them and already in the eye of Time the temples and the sacrifices and the bloody cruelties of Rome were numbered, and the day would come when the city of columns would be reborn into a city of churches. Upon the Appian Way one remembers these words from Acts 28:14-16:

And so we ended our journey at Rome. The brethren there, who had heard our story, came out as far as Appius' Forum, and on to the Three Taverns, to meet us; Paul gave thanks to God and took courage when he saw them.

Once we were in Rome, Paul was allowed to have his own residence, which he shared with the soldier who guarded him.

31

So the figures of the great Apostles pass on along the Appian Way to the Eternal City. "For these, O Rome, are the men through whom the light of Christ's Gospel shone upon thee, when she, who was the mistress of error became the disciple of truth. They are thy holy Fathers and true Pastors, having with better and happier omens founded thee for a place in the heavenly kingdom, than those who laid the first stones of thy walls. . . ."[3]

The Bishop and the boy bent down and touched the stones of the old road before they went back into Rome.

FORUM ROMANUM

From the back of the Senators' Palace upon the Capitoline Hill you can look down into the heart of ancient Rome. You see the Forum Romanum below you, from the Arch of Septimius Severus to the Arch of Titus, and the vista closes with the immense curve of the hideous Colosseum. It is curious to think how that monster has endeared itself to the world. Not only was it consecrated to blood, cruelty and the bestiality of an idle mob, but even in the days of its glory, when it was sheeted in marble and covered with statues, it must have been, in its own gigantic way, a worthy ancestor of the Victor Emmanuel Monument. Those who do not admire it are glad to think that its marble has gone to the making of so many lovely Renaissance palaces and churches.

The Forum, on the other hand, is one of the most appealing ruins in the world. It is not beautiful as the Parthenon is beautiful; you

[3] Serm. I *de SS. Apost. Petro et Paulo* (St. Leo the Great preaching at St. Peter's tomb about A.D. 440).

32

do not catch your breath in wonder when you see it first, as if some glorious white bird had suddenly alighted near you; you look at it with much the same sorrow that we of this generation have known in our own cities as, turning a corner, we come upon a scene once noble and dear to us but now flattened by aerial bombardment. Of course no one ever really sees the Forum for the *first* time. We have all seen so many pictures of it in guidebooks and books of travel, we have all been sent a postcard of it "with love from Aunt Agatha," so that to face the reality is rather like meeting an old acquaintance, and perhaps finding him neither so tall nor quite as impressive as we remembered him in years gone by.

The Roman Forum from the Capitoline Hill

The ruins lie twenty and thirty feet beneath the modern pavements, and in May the grass grows lush and green everywhere, and there are numerous fig trees, wild roses, acanthus and one remarkable invader, a wistaria, near the temple of Antoninus and Faustina. It gives one an odd feeling to watch an old man emerge far below and begin to cut the grass with a sickle on a spot near the Curia which the feet of Augustus must have touched many a time.

Most old cities have one place consecrated to the early memories of their citizens, and in Rome this was the Forum Romanum. It was the small level marshy place at the base of two right-angled hills which, tradition says Romulus, when he had made friends with the Sabines, selected as the heart of their united tribal settlement. It was their meeting place and their market; and so it remained throughout history. As time went on, emperor after emperor made it more splendid and even extended it into more lavish, roomier and more wonderful *fora*, such as the Forum of Trajan; but still the affection of Rome clung to the Forum Romanum—the germ cell of the great Empire. The Caesars worked the most precious and remote marble quarries to bring from Greece, Asia Minor and the East enormous blocks of white, pink, green and red marbles to those warehouses of the Tiber. Their memory is still preserved in the name of the Via Marmorata near the site of the ancient docks. The creak of cranes lifting blocks of stone and the chip and tinkle of the stone masons' chisels and hammers must have been the characteristic sounds of Rome for centuries, and in a hundred distant gashes in the earth's crust an unknown and forgotten army of slaves and criminals labored and died, generation after generation, with stone dust in their hair and lungs to satisfy Rome's insatiable appetite for marble.

And most of that marble is still in Rome. It has migrated to the churches and the palaces. The Palazzo Farnese and the Palazzo della Cancellaria were built of Colosseum marble; the red columns of the Fontana Paola came from the Temple of Minerva; the Church of St. Ignatius was built from the Temple of Sacrae Urbis;

the tremendous flight of steps to St. Maria in Aracoeli came from Aurelian's huge Temple of the Sun; the marble of the Trevi Fountain came from the tomb of Caecilia Metella; the Temple of Antoninus and Faustina helped to repair the Lateran, though the superb columns of Carystian marble, which remain, were spared by Pope Urban V because he considered them to be under the protection of St. Lawrence (this did not, however, deter Paul III from taking the steps away from under them for St. Peter's!). And St. Peter's itself is a vast museum of classical marble; even the high altar once formed part of the Temple of Minerva. It would be possible to continue for pages showing how the Rome of the Caesars was lifted out of the brambles and rubbish heaps to become the Rome of the Renaissance Popes. It is an odd thought that the Caesars brought to Rome the marble which the Popes have made into churches; but wherever you look your eyes light upon some column, some architrave, some stairway of pagan Rome now serving a different purpose in Christian Rome.

So, when you stand upon this vantage point on the Capitol and look down at the Forum, you are really looking at an abandoned quarry, and all you see are a few ruins preserved by some accident of fate, or for some other reason, left there by the lime-burner and the architects. How splendid it must have been for so much to have defied Time and to be today sufficiently impressive, lying there amid the grass and red poppies, to stimulate the mind and to make a man think, as he looks down upon it, that no other place of equal area on the earth's surface has known such famous events.

Only with the eye of the mind can one see it now, its streets crowded, statues of marble and of gilded bronze at every corner and mounted upon the roofs, the wide temple steps rising this way and that, the Sacred Way winding down the hill, the tuft of smoke rising from the Temple of Vesta, the gilded tiles catching the morning sun, the litters pressing through the crowds between the tall marble cliffs of the streets (for wheels were forbidden by daylight in the streets of Imperial Rome); and only with the imagination can one see the Temple of Jupiter with its golden roof rising upon

the Capitoline Hill, and people on the adjacent ridge of the Palatine, now gaunt with its brick vaults and stone pines, with glittering palaces lifting themselves terrace upon terrace, each one a display of wealth and luxury never since surpassed by the monarchs of the world.

This was the Rome which St. Peter and St. Paul saw in the full heyday of its pride and power. This was the center of the world. They saw it at a time when the commerce and the wealth of the world were concentrated in it, when the stock exchanges were in action, when great markets displayed the products of distant countries, when messengers passed each other every day on all the great roads, going and coming on the business of the Empire. We must imagine the Apostles in the Forum in a scene not unlike that of any bustling street market of modern Rome—the Campo dei Fiori, for instance—where people of all types and races pushed and shouted and sold things against a background of immense dignity and austerity. Only fourteen years after their martyrdom the Emperor Domitian issued a bylaw in an attempt to stop the historic Roman tendency to overflow upon the pavement; and a poet wrote, "Thanks to you, Germanicus, no pillar is now girt with chained flagons . . . nor does the grimy cook-shop monopolize the public way. Barber, tavern-keeper, cook and butcher keep within their own threshold. Now Rome exists, which so recently was one vast shop."[4]

We think of the Forum in ancient times as a splendid place inhabited by stately figures in white; splendid it certainly was, but the populace hung bottles on the columns and shaved each other in the marble streets! That is life as it really was rather than as we imagine it to have been. Into this coarse, thrusting Rome, with its extremes of wealth and poverty, ancient, powerful and seemingly immortal, passed Peter and Paul, glancing around at the fabulous wealth of the Caesars, the mighty monuments of the pagan world, a great proportion of the columns and the temples of which would one day be carried away to be transformed into churches.

[4] Martial VII. 61.

The pilgrim who descends into the Forum naturally asks himself what existing ruins the eyes of the Apostles might have seen; and the answer is "hardly any." Perhaps the three remaining superb columns of the Temple of Castor and Pollux, which date from the restoration under Augustus, are the only objects they saw which we can still see. The Colosseum was not built, neither was the Arch of Titus nor any of the buildings whose ruins are scattered on either side of the Sacra Via. But they did see the first-century predecessors of these buildings, erected on the same sites but rebuilt and reconstructed time and again until the last age of the Empire. They must, for instance, have stood before the Temple of Julius Caesar, which now is merely a brick core stripped of all its marble. They must have heard the story of Caesar's cremation at the hands of the crowd at that very spot; of Mark Antony's oration and his reading of Caesar's will, just as they must have gazed at the Rostrum, whose superstructure still exists; they must have seen the Senate House, the Curia—a word which was to migrate to the Vatican Hill—whose successor of Diocletian's time is still standing, built on the same site.

Paganism lingered long among the aristocracy of Rome, for its vested interests were great and powerful and the Church was poor. A public man, or one who had his way to make up the administrative ladder, his *cursus honorum*, found it essential to pay homage to the official gods, no matter how formal and casual this may have been; but the Christian conscience could not be reconciled to such an attitude. Martyrs died rather than cast a pinch of incense on a pagan altar. Such considerations did not, however, affect the wives of Roman officials and public men, and that is one of the reasons why the names of so many more aristocratic women than men appear in the early history of the Church.

Another survival of supreme interest to pilgrims in the Forum is the Arch of Titus, which was set up to commemorate the end of the Jewish War in 70 A.D. and the destruction of Jerusalem under Titus. Speaking of Jerusalem, our Lord said,

The Colosseum

Thy enemies will fence thee round about, and encircle thee, and press thee hard on every side, and bring down in ruin both thee and thy children that are in thee, not leaving one stone of thee upon another (Luke 19:43-44).

This was a literal description of the military operation which led to the destruction of the city. First, the Romans dug an immense trench all round Jerusalem, then the legions waited behind it until the city starved. When the final assault came, Titus was anxious to save the Temple of Herod but someone threw a torch into it and the building was destroyed by accident. The bas-reliefs on the inside of the Arch prove that the famous objects in the Holy of Holies were saved and were sent to Rome: the seven-branched candlestick, two censers, two long trumpets, the Ark of the Covenant. These are all sculptured upon the arch, but Josephus says that, in addition, the Veil of the Temple and the Books of the Law were also sent to Rome.

The sculptures also feature a figure which no one ever notices. It is that of an aged man with a long beard who is carried in a litter. This was the traditional manner in which the Romans pictured a river, or the river god, a venerable and bearded version of Neptune. This particular old gentleman is the Jordan.

What happened to the treasures of the Temple is a mystery. Procopius says that they were looted from the Temple of Peace in the Forum by the Goths and the Vandals in two separate raids, that the Vandals shipped their share of the treasure to Carthage where it was later found by Belisarius and sent to Constantinople. The Jews of Rome apparently never believed this story, probably because the Talmud says the treasure was flung into the Tiber. They believed until comparatively recent times that it still lay there, perhaps buried deep in mud and maybe swept down towards Ostia in the course of the centuries; however, as recently as the eighteenth century the Jews of Rome petitioned the reigning Pope to have the Tiber dredged in the hope of discovering the seven-branched candlestick and the Ark.

42

Fishpond, Garden of the Vestal Virgins

Perhaps the most appealing of all pagan memorials in the Forum is the House of the Vestal Virgins with its row of statues and, nearby, the remains of the beautiful little round temple of the whitest marble, where for centuries the priestesses tended the sacred flame. The House of the Vestals was a large and stately one, paved and decorated with costly marbles, but all signs of its grandeur have long since vanished, leaving only the outline of a large atrium, grass-grown and full of wild roses in early summer, where enormous and voracious goldfish live in oblong pools and eagerly fight for the remains of any breakfast rolls which tourists may bring for them.

43

Many scholars have noted the similarity between the House of the Vestals and the Christian nunnery, and between the rites of admission to the order—a vow of chastity, the cutting-off of hair, the assumption of white garments, and the taking of a new name—with those of Christian monasticism. The memories in the *Atrium Vestæ* are those of paganism at its best, but a few steps away, glimpsed through the Arch of Titus, is that haunted circle of stone, the Colosseum, consecrated to the vile cruelty of the pagan world.

The pilgrim will stand in the Colosseum, saddened by the cruelty it has witnessed and conscious maybe that fear and sorrow seem to have soaked in some way into the fractured brickwork; and he will stand also at the nearby Arch of Constantine, which that Emperor erected to celebrate his victory over Maxentius at the Milvian Bridge, when he entered Rome with his British and German troops, carrying the sign of the Cross upon his banner. This is therefore the

Statue, Garden of the Vestal Virgins

Arch of Constantine

first public Christian monument in the world, and some believe that
the name of Christ is to be seen upon it. The words are INSTINCTU
DIVINITATIS MENTIS MAGNITUDINE, which imply the name
of the Saviour, and proclaimed to the Rome of the Caesars that
Christ had conquered.

Trajan's Column

It may be that as the thoughtful pilgrim wanders the streets of Rome he will wonder how the course of world history might have been altered had any of the great Emperors embraced the Christian Faith—Trajan (A.D. 53-117), Hadrian (A.D. 76-138), or the philosopher, Marcus Aurelius (A.D. 121-180). All three men have left memorials in Rome. Trajan's magnificent Column, covered with military sculpture, stands in the center of his Forum and Market, once the most splendid and fashionable lounging and shopping place in Rome. Today only a ground plan is left to assist the imagination in reconstructing the gilded and gleaming libraries, halls, courts, and statues that stood there, and in the Market itself, once the site of the most exclusive shops, is the largest colony of stray cats in Rome.

The mighty Hadrian has left his name to that circle of red brickwork near St. Peter's—Hadrian's Tomb or the Castel San Angelo—which became the fortress of the Popes during the violent Middle Ages. The visitor who climbs the long, inclined ramp up which the Emperor's sarcophagus was pulled may read upon the wall, above the place where his remains once rested, Hadrian's famous "Address to his Soul":

Feeding the cats, Trajan's Market

The Cordonata, Capitoline Hill, leading to the Senate Palace

Genial, little, vagrant sprite,
Long my body's friend and guest,
To what place is now thy flight?
Pallid, stark, and naked quite,
Stripped henceforth of joke and jest.[5]

Of Marcus Aurelius, the author of the famous *Meditations*, we have the only equestrian bronze statue from ancient Roman times. It stands at the top of the long ramp, the Cordonata, that leads up to the Capitoline Hill, where horse and rider, the bronze still touched with gilt, occupy the center of what is perhaps the most dignified piazza in Rome.

All three Emperors were good, compassionate men who pondered the problems of life and after life. Of one of them, Trajan, the pretty medieval story is told that St. Gregory, touched by that Emperor's concern for the poor and for widows, prayed God to open the Christian heaven to him, and, the story goes, God consented.

[5] Translation by Thomas Spencer Jerome in *Roman Memories* (1914).

II
THE ROME OF
THE APOSTLES

THE TITULI

SHOULDERED by modern buildings in the heart of Rome are a number of churches which lie below the street level and may be approached only by flights of steps. They belong, like the Forum, to a world that lived and walked thirty and forty feet beneath the pavements of modern Rome. Several of these churches go back to the time of the Apostles, but they have been rebuilt so often, and so recently, that only a stray column, a mosaic, or a crypt, gives a clue to their astonishing antiquity.

These are the titular churches of Rome. They existed as meeting places for Christians three centuries before St. Peter's and St. Paul's or any public church existed. Beneath their naves you can sometimes see as in St. Pudenziana, the foundation of a first-century Roman building, and far beneath the church of SS. John and Paul upon the Aventine you enter a kind of underground Pompeii and pass through room after room decorated with frescoes painted in the second and third centuries. Many of the *tituli* are older than the catacombs and are the most venerable places of worship in the Western world.

Had we lived as Christians in the Rome of the Apostles we should have known many of these *tituli*, and all our Christian friends would have been aware of them too. Until the first persecution under Nero there was probably no secret about them, but when Christians had attracted the attention of the police a blanket of silence and mystery descended upon them and the faithful went to them in secret and did not talk about them for fear of implicating the owners, whose names they bore.

They were private houses often belonging to Romans of wealth and consequence and were known in that age before martyrs by the *titulus*, or title, of the householder. There was a *titulus Pudentis*, a *titulus Vestinae*, named after a Roman lady called Vestina; a *titulus Equitii*, from a priest named Equitius; a *titulus Lucinae*—another Roman matron—a *titulus Tigridae*, and so on.

In the earliest times the buildings were known as the *domus Dei*, then later they were called *Dominicum*. The most ancient name for a Christian church which survives is the Italian word for a cathedral, *duomo*. The ancient word also appears in the name of one church in Rome, St. Maria in Dominica, on the highest point of the Caelian Hill.

After the Peace of the Church in A.D. 312 the titular churches were placed in charge of a priest who became known as *presbyter cardinalis*, from *cardo*, a hinge, or the priest upon whom everything turns; and so the pattern of the Roman parish churches evolved. Nowadays every member of the College of Cardinals is the "titular" of one or another of these ancient churches. Their heraldic shields are displayed above the doors and their portraits in oils are hung in the churches, while the red hats of departed titulars are allowed to moulder, a prey to damp and moth, from the roofs of chapels. In such ways the Church with its incredible memory, the longest corporate memory in the world today, keeps an appointment with its past.

It is curious to reflect that neither St. Peter nor St. Paul ever saw anything resembling our conception of a church. They never saw a reliquary or probably a permanent altar. They knew the church simply as a group of Christians who met in a certain house for teaching, baptism, and the celebration of the Holy Eucharist. When they referred to it they called it a "house." "My greetings to Prisca and Aquila" wrote St. Paul, " . . . [and] to the congregation which meets in their house" and again, "greet . . . Nymphas, [and the] church that is in his *household*."

One thinks of the house in Jerusalem in which our Lord gathered his disciples for the Last Supper, a house which was to be re-created in Rome wherever St. Peter said Mass; a house that was to descend into the tomb of the Catacombs and to be resurrected into the light of day upon the Vatican Hill and the road to Ostia. Historians have traced the history of the church to the *tituli* and the catacombs. But its tradition goes back beyond them to the House of the Upper Chamber in Jerusalem in which the Last Supper was held, where Jesus appeared to His followers, to which St. Peter fled after his deliverance from prison and in which the miracle of Pentecost occurred. This was truly the Mother Church of Christendom and the *tituli* of Rome, the rooms in which St. Peter and St. Paul ministered and preached, were its descendants. Though the glittering shrines of Christianity, which owe their fame to the older cult of martyrs, have taken the world's attention from these often humble and frequently not very architecturally attractive buildings, they remain to the thoughtful Christian infinitely the most interesting and moving objects in Rome.

St. Pudenziana is the most notable of all the titular churches. It is the house which Cardinal Wiseman, who took his title from it, believed was the house where St. Paul lodged with the Senator Pudens and where St. Peter erected his chair as Bishop of Rome. As the tradition which links this church with St. Peter dates from the fourth century, there is every reason to believe this building to be the cradle of the Church.

It stands a short distance from St. Mary Major in a busy street, and, having descended the steps which lead down to it, the stranger

53

Looking down at the house of Pudens, Church of St. Pudenziana

sees nothing at first save the superb fresco in the apse. This glorious glowing picture dates from about A.D. 390 and shows the Saviour dressed as a Roman senator in a golden toga with a blue stripe. He holds an open book upon whose pages may be read the words *Dominus conservator ecclesiae Pudentianae*[1] and His attitude is that of a Roman judge or magistrate. Grouped on either side are St. Peter and St. Paul, and in the corners are two women, St. Pudenziana and her sister St. Prassede, holding wreaths. These early representations of the Apostles follow the traditional portraits as seen in the Vatican Museum in the bases of the *vetri cemeteriali*, the little glasses discovered in great numbers in the catacombs, with pictures of the Apostles stamped in gold leaf in the bases. The type never alters. St. Peter has a strong, full face and his hair is short and curly; St. Paul is leaner, rather wiry and bald. Those who have studied this subject believe that the portraits embody a tradition which had been current in the Church from the first century and is derived from those who knew the Apostles when they were alive.

An excavation in the nave of St. Pudenziana has been left exposed so that the visitor can see beneath the church the remains of a Roman house and a heating system of the first century. Here were found innumerable bones evidently gathered from the catacombs during the barbarian invasions. Let into an altar is a piece of ancient wood protected by a sheet of plate glass. This is a piece of wood that has been treasured for centuries in St. Pudenziana as a portion of the portable altar, or table, on which St. Peter said Mass. The table itself, or rather what is left of it, is enclosed within the high altar of St. John Lateran. When Cardinal Wiseman was titular cardinal of St. Pudenziana he had the fragment of wood in his church scientifically examined together with the wood in the Lateran, and the report was that both came from the same table. The Cardinal then had the fragment at St. Pudenziana enclosed in the altar.

The family of Pudens appears to have formed the nucleus of the Christian Church in Rome in apostolic times. Quintus Cornelius

---

[1] *The Lord, Preserver of the Pudentian Church.*

Inside the Church of SS. John and Paul

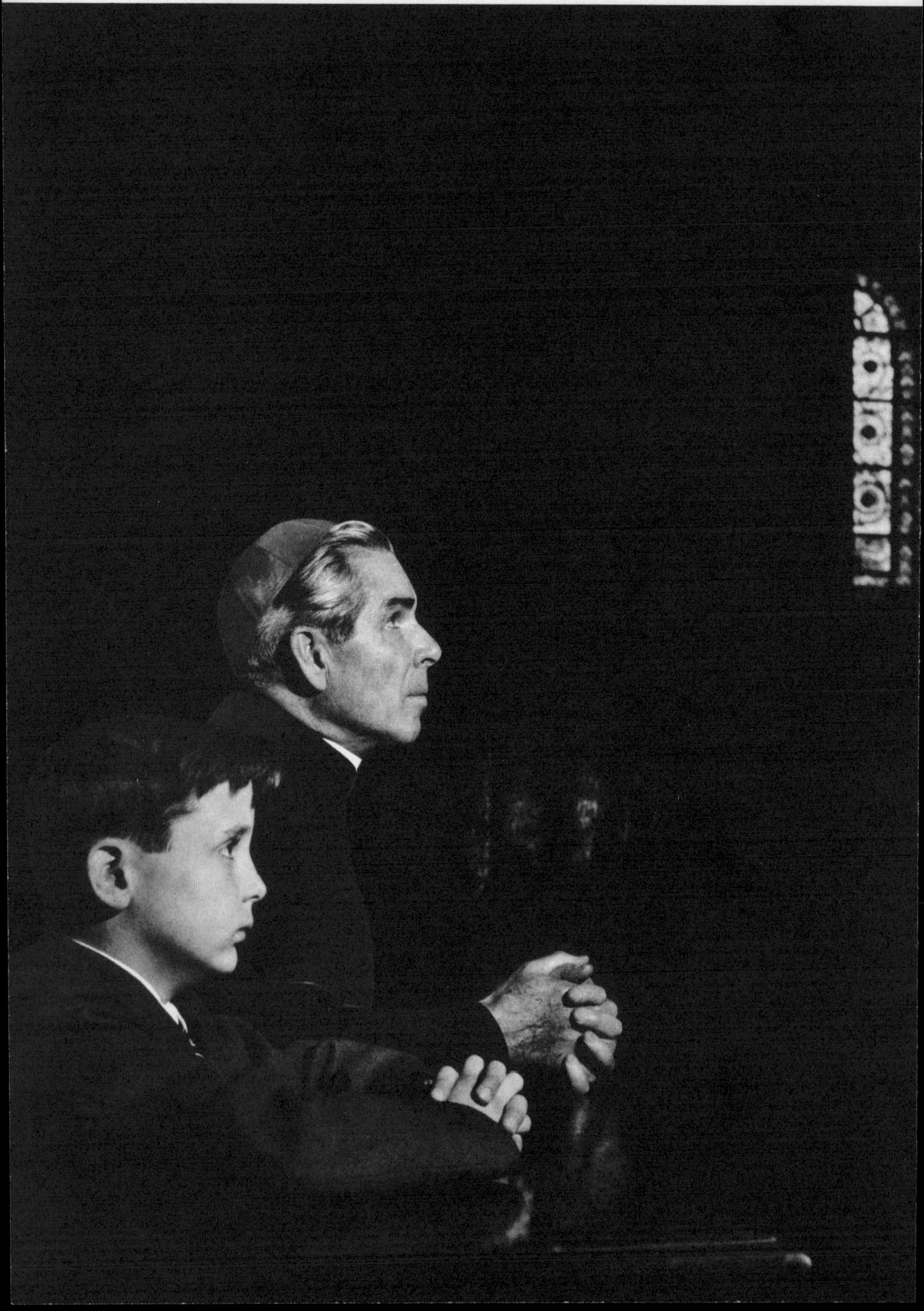

Pudens, was a member of the Senate and was married to a lady of ample means named Priscilla. Their son, also Quintus Cornelius Pudens and also a convert, married Claudia Rufina, whom many believe to have been a Briton and the bride mentioned by Martial in one of his epigrams. It has been suggested that she was the daughter of the British chief, Caractacus, who with his wife and daughters was taken as captive to Rome after the Claudian invasion of Britain and eventually set at liberty.

Although the pilgrim is obliged to see the antiquity of St. Pudenziana with the eye of faith, it is otherwise with the beautiful church of SS. John and Paul on the Aventine. This old church, whose titular is Cardinal Spellman, is the mother-house of the Passionist Fathers, who have an adjacent monastery which covers a part of the hill where in imperial times the menagerie of the Colosseum was housed and where water was stored for naval contests in the amphitheater. The church is a beautiful one, and is especially brilliant, gay and happy when hanging festoons of some thirty crystal chandeliers are lighted; a reason maybe why it is one of the four most popular churches for weddings in Rome. The others are: St. Frances in the Forum, St. Cecilia in Trastevere and St. Gregory the Great on the Caelian. It was in SS. John and Paul that Bishop Fulton Sheen was consecrated Bishop on June 11, 1951, by Adeodato Cardinal Piazza, with Archbishop Leo Negris and Bishop Martin O'Connor as co-consecrators.

A Passionist opens a door into a cold tunnel that leads beneath the church, where two Roman houses of the fourth century are revealed, with frescoes as fresh and bright upon the walls as if in Herculaneum. In the descent of those steps sixteen centuries are abolished, and the amazed pilgrim finds himself in a scene where time apparently has been standing still. Even the wine jars were found stacked in the wine cellar.

The house belonged to two prosperous Romans, John and Paul, who refused to take an official position under Julian the Apostate and make the necessary sacrifice to Jupiter. They were given ten

Outside the Church of
SS. John and Paul

days to reconsider their decision, a time they spent in setting their affairs in order, disposing of their fortune, and in prayer. At the end of the time they were beheaded and their bodies flung into a pit hastily dug under the stairs, while a report was circulated to the effect that they had been sent into exile. But fellow Christians knew what had happened, and after Julian's death the house was turned into a sanctuary but was filled in with earth later and a church built on top of it.

In the last century rationalists claimed that no such persons as SS. John and Paul had ever existed. This inspired a Passionist, Father Germano, to dig under the church where he was convinced that the Roman house, long filled in and forgotten, would be discovered. He began his excavations in 1887, and was able to clear room after room of the rubbish and debris piled into them, and eventually he and his successors revealed two Roman houses in a marvelous state of preservation. It is one of the most revealing of all the *tituli* in Rome, showing how the original *titulus*, becoming

58

too small for the worshipers, was abandoned in favor of a new building erected on top of it.

Much the same thing is to be seen in that exquisite church of St. Clement near the Colosseum where two churches may be visited, one on top of the other, the lower one taking us back almost to Apostolic times. This was the *dominicum* of St. Clement, possibly the actual house, as tradition asserts, of the third occupant of the Papacy. Not only is St. Clement the most beautiful of all Rome's medieval churches, and a perfect kaleidoscope of Cosmatesque marbles, but it is also an ideal example of the phoenixlike history of the *tituli*.

Another type is architecturally deceptive such as St. Susanna in the Via Venti Settembre, which anyone would accept at a glance as just another baroque church. But a Roman house was discovered beneath it in recent times in which it is believed Gabinus, the brother of Pope Caius (A.D. 283), was martyred with his daughter, Susanna, during Diocletian's persecution. It is possible to descend into this crypt and examine the rooms which adjoined a stretch of the old Servian Wall. St. Susanna's also commemorates an unusual saint, Genesius, the patron saint of actors. He is said to have been the leading comedian of his day, and while making fun of Christ and Christianity upon the stage was suddenly and unexpectedly converted, and died, also under Diocletian, for his faith. Genesius is among the saints sculptured on Bernini's colonnade round St. Peter's and, when pictured in art, which, however, is rather rare, he is shown wearing cap and bells.

In 1922, St. Susanna's became the American church in Rome and was placed in the kindly hands of the Paulist Fathers, who upon the first Sunday in the month welcome every American Catholic in Rome to the ten o'clock Mass, after which an American breakfast is served.

The *tituli* are many and varied. They have only one thing in common: their roots go down into the Rome of the Apostles, or to a time during the first three centuries A.D. before the existence of any public churches.

59

Pulpit of St. Lawrence-Outside-the-Walls

III
THE ROME OF
THE PILGRIMS

THE SEVEN CHURCHES

A CENTURY before Christianity was a tolerated religion, pilgrims set out to see for themselves the scenes associated with our Lord's ministry and crucifixion, and also the tombs of St. Peter and St. Paul. They traveled in a spirit of serious inquiry, as any scholar might do today, and they saw the holy places at a time when human links still existed with the Apostolic age.

The first recorded pilgrim was Alexander, the friend of Origen, who went to Jerusalem in A.D. 212 "for the sake of prayer and the investigation of the places." Origen himself followed twice, first in A.D. 216 and again in A.D. 231. In those times the pilgrim in the Holy Land saw infinitely less than we do today. Jerusalem, after having been laid waste by Titus in A.D. 70, had remained in ruins until Hadrian saw it in the second century and ordered the superb site to be occupied with a city to be called Aelia Capitolina, a conjunction of his own name, Aelius, with that of the god, Jupiter Capitolinus. The new Jerusalem, a Roman city of straight streets and marble columns, was dedicated to Jupiter in A.D. 136 and among its new buildings was a Temple of Venus erected upon the hill of Golgotha. That was the Jerusalem seen by Alexander and Origen.

It is tantalizing that these early pilgrims should have left no details of their experiences, which must have been of surpassing interest. It is not beyond the bounds of possibility that in A.D. 212 a centenarian might well have known, in his childhood, an old man whose father, certainly whose grandfather, had heard our Lord preach, or had even been present at the Crucifixion. In the East, where so many events have always been faithfully handed down by word of mouth from one generation to another, the critical and educated visitor, meeting people in Aelia Capitolina centuries before the commercialization of pilgrimage or the multiplication of the holy sites, must have heard much that we would dearly love to know today.

The longing of Christians to draw physically near to the places sanctified by the footsteps of our Lord received its first great impulse in A.D. 326 when that dauntless old lady, the Empress Helena, the mother of Constantine, though nearly eighty years of age, made her pilgrimage to the Holy Land "to pay the debt of pious feeling to God, the King of all." It was during this visit that St. Helena pulled down the Temple of Venus and discovered the True Cross. With the building of the Church of the Holy Sepulchre, in Jerusalem, and the Church of the Nativity, in Bethlehem, the story of Christian pilgrimage leaves the shadows and emerges into the light of history.

It is extraordinarily interesting that Roman pilgrimage began at an equally early time. Pilgrims did not wait for the Peace of the Church before they visited the tombs of the Apostles. They went to Rome a century before there were any public churches and when the Church was confined to the *tituli* and the catacombs. The two great pilgrimage sites were exactly as today—the tombs, or memorials, of St. Peter upon the Vatican Hill and the tomb of St. Paul off the Ostian Way.

In those days the Vatican Hill was a lonely suburban cemetery among whose tombs stood a memorial to which any Christian child in Rome at the time could have directed the pilgrim. The first recorded visitor was a priest named Caius, who lived during the pontificate of St. Zephyrinus (A.D. 199-217), and wrote, perhaps in the year A.D. 220, words which have been preserved by Eusebius. "I can show you," wrote Caius, "the trophies of the Apostles. For if you go to the Vatican or the Ostian Way, there you will find the trophies of those who founded this church." Others who are known to have visited the tomb of St. Peter before any church existed there were St. Paternus, who came from Alexandria in the year A.D. 253; St. Marcius, who came from Persia with his wife and two sons in A.D. 269; and St. Maurus from Africa in A.D. 284. Even in times of persecution, we learn that SS. Constantine and Victoria went immediately they arrived in Rome to pray on the Vatican Hill and were caught there by soldiers and put to death. The same fate overtook St. Zoe, also Tranquillinius.

What form the Vatican "trophy" took has been the subject of much learned debate. What precisely did these first pilgrims see? Most scholars think that St. Peter's tomb was marked by a *cella memoriae* of the type usual in Roman times: a pillaried niche with a pediment standing above ground and probably erected, as stated in the *Liber Pontificalis*, by Pope Anacletus (A.D. 76-88), who had known St. Peter and had been ordained a presbyter by him.

This was the *aedicula*, or shrine, round which St. Peter's was built by Constantine, and in order to preserve it a landscape was altered so that it might rise as the central feature of the church. As the Vatican Hill sloped sharply from north to south, the engineers, taking the shrine as their level, cut away the hill to the north, and built it up to the south, with the same total disregard for difficulties shown by Constantine when he cut away the hill of Golgotha to leave the tomb of our Lord as a detached rock in the first church of the Holy Sepulchre. The same principles were observed upon the Ostian Way in building the first Constantinian basilica of St. Paul's.

The ruins of St. Peter's "trophy" still exist directly underneath the high altar of the present basilica, and were seen and examined for the first time since the fourth century in 1940, when, with the approval of Pius XII, the excavations were started which have laid bare what is the most marvelous sight in Rome: the street of the pagan and Christian cemetery in which St. Peter was buried.

It is difficult for the visitor in St. Peter's to think of anything as simple as the extraordinary scene that lies in the darkness beneath his feet. He is stunned by splendor. He is surrounded by grandeur so gigantic that even cherubs at the holy water stoups are at least six feet high. But it is good in that place for him to shut his eyes to the magnificence of Bernini's baldacchino, even to the miracle of Michelangelo's dome above it, and to reflect that he stands at a spot where a humble grave once lay in the sunlight and under the stars, a grave which Christians venerate as the resting place of the Prince of the Apostles since the time of Nero.

The building of the first basilicas in the time of Constantine attracted to Rome pilgrims from all parts of the Christian world. There are two distinct phases in the history of Roman pilgrimage; the first lasted from the time of Constantine until the barbarian invasions of the fifth–eighth centuries. In the first phase pilgrims made their devotions at the tombs of St. Peter and St. Paul, which, though miles apart, were linked by a superb colonnade of marble columns with a leaden roof beneath which the pilgrims walked dry shod. Afterwards they went out to pray in the catacombs. Lamps were kept burning before the tombs of the saints and Mass was said on the tombs or nearby.

During this period the pilgrims let down bits of cloth to the tombs of St. Peter and St. Paul through apertures made specially for this purpose. The tomb of St. Peter lay at the bottom of a vertical shaft which was twice interrupted by perforated plates called *cataractae* that prevented objects from dropping down upon it. Objects placed upon the lower of these plates gained great virtue as relics, though the ordinary pilgrim who lowered his scarf or handkerchief was, of course, able only to touch the first of the plates. When the Emperor Justinian asked for actual bodily relics for a new church he was building in Constantinople, and had been refused by Pope

Hormisdas, he begged humbly that objects might be sent to him which, if possible, had been placed upon the lower of the two plates —*ad cataractam secundam.*

The pilgrims took away from Rome, in addition to cloths, called *brandea*, which had been in contact with the Apostolic tombs, little glass bottles and phials of pottery or metal containing oil from the catacombs. A wonderful collection from that remote age is still to be seen in the treasury of the Cathedral at Monza, in Lombardy, where many oil bottles still remain from a collection of seventy sent to Queen Theodolina in the time of St. Gregory the Great (A.D. 590-604), each one labeled with the name of the saint from whose tomb the oil had been gathered.

This was the period when the Popes sternly rebuked those who asked for bones and actual portions of a saint's body, telling them not only of the wickedness, but of the physical peril, of disturbing God's elect.

The second phase of pilgrimage came after the barbarian invasions when, after the catacombs had been sacked by successive waves of Goths, Vandals, Lombards, and Saracens, the bones of the martyrs were taken into the churches of Rome. Boniface IV carried twenty-eight wagon-loads of bones from the catacombs in A.D. 609 and placed them beneath the Pantheon, which he consecrated as a church under the name of St. Maria ad Martyres, and a more selective translation was begun under Pope Honorius and was continued by successive Popes until Rome's dwindling population of the living must almost have been outnumbered by the population of the dead which now invaded every church. In Constantine's day a church had only one altar, but with the great influx of saints in the Dark Ages numerous side altars were erected in order that the martyrs might be venerated.

In this period the pilgrim took away, not oil bottles and *brandea*, but human bones and tissue; and so began that traffic in relics which reached such extravagant proportions in the Middle Ages. In the earlier times the value of a relic was the devotion it inspired in its

Dome, St. Pete

possessor, not in the relic itself as a possible source of supernatural energy.

So the pilgrim in the Rome of the Middle Ages found himself in a city of saints. The catacombs had given up their dead and the pilgrim could have spent many months in venerating all the shrines. Thus a pattern of pilgrimage was evolved that remains the same today as it was centuries ago. This is a tour of the Seven Churches of Rome. These are: St. Peter's, St. Paul's-Outside-the-Walls, St. Mary Major, St. John Lateran, Holy Cross in Jerusalem, St. Lawrence-Outside-the-Walls, and St. Sebastian upon the Appian Way.

Near the Lateran, in a separate building, is the Scala Santa—the Holy Staircase—whose twenty-eight marble steps became so worn

St. Paul's-Outside-the-Walls

Façade, St. Paul's-Outside-the-Walls

into holes and hollows by the knees of pilgrims that Clement XII (1730-1740) preserved them with a wooden covering that has been renewed several times since the eighteenth century. Tradition says that these steps were brought from the palace of Pilate in Jerusalem in the fourth century by St. Helena, the mother of Constantine the Great, and they are believed to be those which Christ descended wearing the Crown of Thorns. Pilgrims have been ascending these

71

Borghese Chapel, St. Mary Major

72

steps upon their knees for sixteen centuries, and today they still do so, especially during Lent and on Good Friday.

So the pilgrim's path in Rome was mapped out centuries ago, and every day they may be seen setting off, not with pilgrim staff and shoon, but in motor coach and automobile, to make their round of the Seven Churches. To the pilgrim of yesterday one of the most venerated of the Seven Churches was St. Sebastian above the Catacomb called "ad catacumbas."

"AD CATACUMBAS"

A FRANCISCAN friar leads the way into the darkness of the Catacomb. Above is the church of St. Sebastian, a building that was, alas, reconstructed in 1612 and every vestige of its antiquity destroyed. But the friar, in passing, indicates a model of the fourth-century basilica as it existed in all its primitive dignity and beauty.

In the ambulatory beneath the apse of the church is a museum of funerary inscriptions discovered during excavations in the catacombs. Some are in Latin, some in Greek, some are misspelled, which somehow seems to bring one touchingly close to those far-off humble Christians who were more accustomed to fetching and carrying than to literary composition. One inscription in particular holds the attention. It states that a certain Eusebius of Antioch, at the age of seventy, had bought a burial plot in the catacombs from a friend of his who was a *fossor*. It is interesting to come across a reference to the *fossores*, who were a guild or union of men who excavated the catacombs from the first century onward. There is a fresco in the Catacomb of St. Callistus which shows a *fossor* named Diogenes in his working clothes, an early Christian version of overalls or jeans. He grasps a pick, while various other implements lie

74

Doors from the Roman Forum, St. John Lateran

Good luck coins
on the tomb of
Pope Martin V,
St. John Lateran

around him, each one a special kind of tool designed to make it easier to work in the narrow tunnels and hew the volcanic tufa. These men were really miners, and they must have had remarkable, and perhaps inherited skill, in order to drive their galleries so accurately, one level on top of the other, all the time keeping the complex system accurately within the prescribed area of the land above.

The catacombs were not haphazard tunnels driven here and there and in any direction, but were carefully planned and subject to bylaws and regulations. As it was an offense to undermine adjacent property, those who made the catacombs had to take care not to commit an act of subterranean trespass.

The tenacious belief that they were secret places is probably due to the many novels and films in which members of the early Church are seen hiding in the catacombs from their persecutors.

At the top of the Scala Santa

That this occurred is beyond question, but the catacombs were all well known to the Roman authorities. It would be no more possible to hide a catacomb than a lead mine. The amount of excavated tufa carried to the surface must have formed dumps above ground visible to all.

Even familiarity cannot diminish the sense of awe and wonder which the catacombs inspire in the mind of anyone who has explored them, and no matter how many times one has descended into that chilly silence which is blacker than blackness, one's first impression remains: that these complex tunnels are among the most astonishing relics of the past to come down to us complete with their inscriptions, with their primitive frescoes, which are the first expression of Christian art; and even with the skeletons of those who were laid to rest there so many ages ago. Father Marchi estimated that some six million Christians were buried in the catacombs, and that if the galleries could be placed end on end they would stretch for six hundred miles. There are about fifty catacombs in a circle round Rome and new ones are frequently discovered. In spite of the barbarian invasions and the wholesale manner in which

Reflection of the façade, Holy Cross in Jerusalem

Piece of the True Cross discovered by St. Helena
(and other relics), Holy Cross in Jerusalem

the bones of the early Christians were taken into Rome to save them
from desecration, numerous tombs are untouched, and many early
Christians sleep peacefully as they were laid to rest so long ago.
Many a visitor has been startled when, shining a flashlight into a
hole in the marble face of a tomb, he looks at a complete skeleton
lying there in the dust of ages!

One descends beneath the church and comes into a dark chamber hewn out of the volcanic tufa. This was the assembly room excavated in 1915 by two archaeologists, A. de Waal and P. Styer, whose
discoveries gave startling confirmation to the ancient tradition of

79

the Church that from the third century onwards this was among the most sacred pilgrim sites in Rome, where the bodies of St. Peter and St. Paul had been hidden at the second milestone upon the Appian Way. The walls of the chamber are covered with scribbling left by ancient pilgrims and preserved now by sheets of plate glass. One shines lights upon them and attempts to read them. Some are in Latin and some in Greek, and they are all simple prayers or invocations, such as "Peter and Paul remember us," or "pray for us," or "help Primus, a sinner," or "preserve Vincentius." They are immensely interesting and immensely touching.

It is tantalizing to think that in spite of this great discovery— perhaps more interesting than any recent discovery in Rome except the excavation beneath St. Peter's—we should still be in the dark about the circumstances in which, and the time when, the bodies of the Apostles were hidden. Already there is a large and conflicting literature on this problem. The most valuable information remains the letter which Gregory the Great wrote to the Byzantine Empress, Constantina, who had asked him for "the head of the holy Paul, or some other bodily relic," telling her of the frightful danger of disturbing a saint's bones. He wrote that "when my predecessor, of blessed memory (Pelagius II), was desirous of changing the silver which was over the most sacred body of the blessed Apostle Peter, although at a distance of almost fifteen feet from the same body, a sign of no small dreadfulness appeared to him." He adds that in years gone by "certain believers from the East" had come to Rome and had managed to steal the Apostles from their tombs on the Vatican Hill and the Via Ostiensis. They managed to carry them as far as the second milestone on the Appian Way, where the thieves fled in terror from a storm of thunder and lightning, abandoning the bodies, which were then recovered by the Roman Christians.

Unfortunately for the modern historian, St. Gregory was not interested in documenting a fact well known to the Church at that time but in impressing upon the imperial lady the danger of relic-hunting. Consequently the date when the bodies of the Apostles

Altar, St. Lawrence

were stolen by the men from the East is open to several interpretations. Some believe that the theft occurred soon after the martyrdom of St. Peter and St. Paul during the Neronian persecution, and there is a tenacious tradition that the bodies remained hidden in a dried-up well on the Via Appia for a year and seven months. Just over fifty years ago this dried-up well was discovered in precisely the spot where the traditions of the Church located it; and to this one descends by way of a long flight of rough damp steps.

One stands in a high tomb chamber, about the size of a large modern room, decorated with traces of first-century stucco work which the damp has not entirely destroyed. Lying one above the other like berths in a liner are tombs or *loculi*, mere shelves in the face of the sepulcher just large enough to take a body. In some of these are bones and skulls with white teeth still in them. Leading from this rock chamber is a narrow entrance to the dry well which was claimed by the long memory of the Church as the spot where the bodies of St. Peter and St. Paul were hidden *Ad Catacumbas*, "in the hollow," on the Appian Way.

Though the excavations which have revealed this spot did not take place until modern times, it was seen with the eye of faith by many saints. St. Philip Neri used to spend whole nights in prayer in the catacomb above, and on one occasion he remained there without food for three days and nights. While he prayed there before the feast of Pentecost a luminous sphere like a globe of light entered his breast and ever afterwards he was conscious of the swelling,

Model, original Church of St. Sebastian

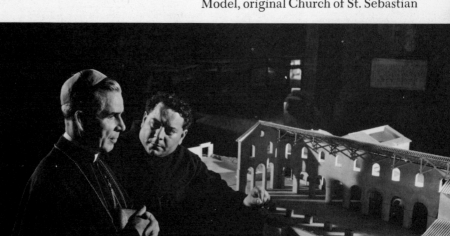

Ancient inscriptions, museum adjoining St. Sebastian

particularly when saying Mass or giving absolution. After his death it was discovered that two of his ribs had parted as if to allow more room for the beating of his heart.

St. Charles Borromeo was another saint who was in the habit of spending entire nights in prayer above this rock chamber. The dark tomb has a place apart in the story of Roman pilgrimage, sanctified, as it is, by a tradition that extends back to the earliest ages.

Modern pilgrims are hurried through in chattering groups while a light is shone down the steps in the direction of the chamber. They go away, glad to be on their way up to the sunlight, unaware that they have so casually dismissed something which the devout of other ages, traveling on foot and on horseback across plain and mountain, facing the dangers of the road and the rigors of the climate, placed among their most precious memories of Rome.

83

THE TOMB CHAPEL

OF THE POPES

ONE day in 1849 a young archaeologist, Giovanni Battista de Rossi, discovered in the cellar of a vineyard on the Appian Way a fragment of marble bearing the letters NELIUS MARTYR. Though only twenty-seven years of age, De Rossi already possessed the scholarship, the imagination and the ingenuity which were to make him the father of modern Christian archaeology. Indeed he seems to have been born an archaeologist. His eleventh birthday present was Antonio Bosio's *La Roma Sotterranea*, and three years later he attracted the attention of the celebrated Cardinal Mai, the Librarian of the Holy Roman Church, who was fascinated to observe a boy of fourteen copying Greek inscriptions in the Vatican. Before he was thirty De Rossi was the inseparable companion, despite the disparity in their ages, of the famous archaeologist, Father Marchi, whose discoveries in underground Rome he was destined to continue and surpass.

As De Rossi held the fragment of marble in his hand, he wondered if it could be a portion of the tombstone of St. Cornelius, the Pope who was martyred in A.D. 253 and buried in the neighborhood of the lost Catacomb of St. Callistus. Strange, indeed incredible, as it may seem, every catacomb in Rome with the exception of *Ad Catacumbas* (St. Sebastian) had been lost during the early Middle Ages, their entrances clogged with debris and covered with vegetation. A number were found by accident during the Renaissance, but many others, like that of St. Callistus, remained unknown until the nineteenth century. The more De Rossi considered his problem, the more he became convinced that the fragment of marble was a clue to the lost catacomb; and his confidence was such that he persuaded Pius IX to buy the vineyard. He was then able to carry on his investigations without hindrance. He was soon rewarded by the three letters COR, which enabled him to complete the name of Pope Cornelius, and eventually he discovered the catacomb, the first man for many centuries to see the Tomb Chapel of the Popes and the tomb of St. Cecilia. Our own century has known some wonderful archaeological discoveries, such as the Tomb of Tut-ankh-Amen and the Burial Pit at Ur of the Chaldees, but nothing we have discovered approaches in human interest and importance the resurrection of this ancient Christian cemetery with its bodies, its tombs, its inscriptions, and its pictures.[1]

The Salesian Fathers, who have succeeded the Trappists as the curators of this catacomb, take one down to the high vaulted Chapel of the Popes, which is a tiny church and one of the most awe-inspiring in Rome. Rising, tier upon tier all round, are the tombs of martyred Popes who reigned during the persecutions that preceded the Peace of the Church. Several of the names are in Greek—Eutychianos, Lokanos, Fabianos, Antheros—a reminder that the Gospels were written in Greek and that Greek was the first language of the Church.

There is perhaps no other spot in Rome in which it is easier to visualize the life of the persecuted Church. The atmosphere of the crypt, the eerie light that falls upon the dusty scene from the *luminaria*, the tunnels that branch off in all directions, and the silence, remind one of St. Jerome's description of his timid explorations of the catacombs while a schoolboy in Rome. Here in these dark mazes is the Golgotha of the Church; the sepulcher from which it rose from the dead into the light of day.

An altar stands in the crypt at which visiting priests are sometimes privileged to say Mass, and above is the finest of the famous inscriptions, in which Pope Damasus (366-384) describes how he cleared the catacombs from the rubbish that had encumbered them

[1] Northcote and Brownlow's *Roma Sotteranea* (1869) is an English abridgment of De Rossi's massive four-volume Italian work, *La Roma Sotterranea Cristiana*.

and how he restored the tombs of the martyrs. This inscription ends
with the beautiful lines:

> *Hic fateor Damasus volui mea condere membra,*
> *Sed cineres timui sanctos vexare Piorum.*[2]

The graceful lettering, inspired by the monumental inscriptions
of Imperial Rome, is the finest calligraphy until the Renaissance,
and was the work of the Pope's secretary, Furiosus Dionysius
Filocalus.

When De Rossi had discovered the papal crypt he found next
to it an empty tomb which he recognized as that from which Pope
Paschal I (817-824) had taken the body of the gentle patron saint
of music, St. Cecilia, and translated it to her church in Trastevere.
Four centuries separate the work of Pope Damasus and that of Pope
Paschal, and again the catacombs had fallen into ruin, this time as
a result of the barbarian invasions. In the year he became Pope,
Paschal took the bodies of twenty-three hundred martyrs from
the catacombs into the safety of the churches of Rome, but he
was unable to find the tomb of St. Cecilia. Eventually he gave up
the attempt in despair, but at that very moment the Saint herself
appeared to him in a dream and told him that while he had been
busy in the crypt of the Popes, he had been within speaking distance
of her. Paschal at once hurried to the catacomb and found the saint's
body "as fresh and perfect as when it was first laid in the tomb, and
clad in rich garments interwoven with gold, with linen cloths
stained with blood rolled up at her feet, lying in a cypress coffin."
Such is the Pope's own description and he adds that he covered the
body with silk, and spread over it a covering of silk gauze before
he laid it in a sarcophagus of white marble and put it under the altar
of the Church of St. Cecilia in Trastevere.[3]

[2] Here I, Damasus, wished to have laid my limbs,
But feared to disturb the holy ashes of the Saints.
[3] Northcote: *Roma Sotteranea*, p. 155.

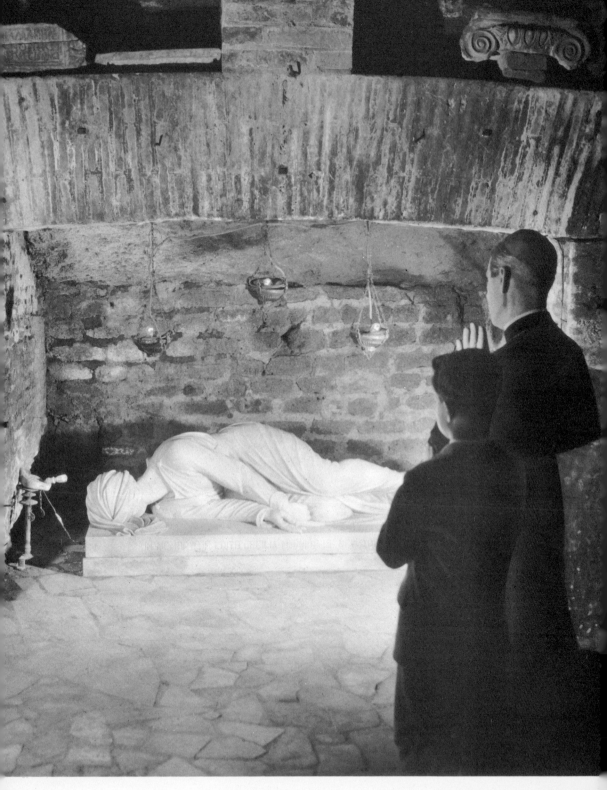

Statue of St. Cecilia, Catacomb of St. Callistus

Seven hundred and eighty-two years passed by, and once again the body of St. Cecilia was seen when Cardinal Sfondrati constructed a new altar in this church. Having seen the Saint lying as if asleep, he immediately called Maderno, the leading sculptor of the day, and asked him to reproduce the incorrupt body in marble. The original is in Trastevere, a copy is in the catacomb, and the visitor, emerging from a gloomy gallery, comes with a start of surprise upon this lifelike figure of a graceful girl sleeping peacefully in the depths of the earth. But a second glance shows something unnatural about the angle of her head. Two other things are noticed: sword cuts upon her neck; and as she died she extended three fingers on the right hand (to signify the Trinity) and two on the left hand (the two Natures, Divine and Human, in Christ).

IV
THE ROME OF
TODAY

SPRING

IN THE month of May Rome is filled with flowers and the crying of swifts as they fly in the evening above the Spanish Steps and the Piazza of St. Peter's. May is the month when winter has definitely departed, and you can see the old ocher-tinted palaces, and the population of gesticulating statues upon the roof-tops gratefully sunning themselves in the returning warmth.

This is the month when the restaurant tables begin to invade the pavement, when the Punch and Judy show appears in the Borghese Gardens and the first rowboats are taken out on the lake there. An air of gaiety and happiness fills the old streets through which uninhibited lovers wander, hand in hand, whispering to each other in a crowd as if alone in a country lane. The Tiber is still high, and its water a grayish-green; nevertheless every bridge has its fringe of optimistic fishermen who let down complicated nets large enough to hold one of Bernini's sea horses; and sometimes, I am told (for I have never been fortunate enough to see this), catch a little fish.

One of the stranger's problems in Rome—how to cross the road— is, of course, insoluble, but a great deal of good will has recently been expended in new traffic lights. There are also policemen who

The Spanish Steps

wear white plastic cuffs, and control the traffic with arms and fingers which positively beseech, plead, flatter, admonish, and rebuke. Those artists direct traffic as a leader conducts an orchestra. The crisp formal movements of ordinary traffic policemen have been elevated by the Italian temperament into an art which is an easily recognizable offshoot of the national language of gesticulation. A quick, scratching movement of white fingers restrains an over-anxious Fiat, just as a conductor might hush a too-zealous cello; and if it ever becomes necessary to use the whole arm several hundred vans, trucks, cars, bicycles, and motor scooters brake in one agonized, unlubricated shriek as suddenly as a drummer muffles his drums at an angry gesture from the conductor.

The sound of water cast up into the spring morning, or gushing downward over rocks, or gently dripping from a marble rim in some silent courtyard, is the voice of Rome. The Emperors brought water to Rome and filled the city with fountains; the Barbarians cut

In the plaza of St. Peter's

Fountain of the Tortoises

the aqueducts but in the fulness of time the Popes restored the water, and also the fountains. No other city can boast so many fountains, neither has any other city encouraged so many great artists to create them. The most famous, of course, is the mighty Trevi, a mountain gorge set in the heart of a city, where Neptune with his sea horses stands triumphantly above the rocky cascade, whose roar can be heard streets away. The fame of the Trevi began over a century ago with the tradition that the traveler who casts a coin into it upon the eve of his departure from Rome will one day return; and in our own time the charming film, *Three Coins in the Fountain*, has brought the old tradition up-to-date and has made the Trevi the most celebrated fountain in the world.

Some, however, may prefer the less spectacular fountains of Rome. For instance, on the edge of the Ghetto, hidden away in a maze of mean streets and enclosed by ancient palaces, is the little Piazza Mattei, whose center is occupied by the exquisite Fountain of the Tortoises. By the standards of Rome it is quite a small one, but it is perfectly satisfying and it expresses the brilliance of the High Renaissance. Its composition, though intricate, gives an impression of absolute simplicity. Four life-sized naked youths, who might perhaps be water sprites, lean against the stem of the fountain, each one grasping the tail of a dolphin with one hand while, with the other, they lift bronze tortoises to the rim of the bowl above them. This beautiful fountain was erected in 1581-1584, during the pontificate of Gregory XIII. The Roman tradition that it was designed by Raphael is a tribute to its beauty, but it is not true; it was built by the Florentine, Taddeo Landini, from a design by Jacoba della Porta.

The streets of Rome are the most varied and characteristic in Europe. If you could cast a net into any crowded thoroughfare and isolate a group of people, you would almost certainly find among them a Franciscan, a Sister of Mercy, a priest, and a seminarist. Never for a moment is one allowed to forget that Rome is the headquarters and the university of the Catholic Church.

One of the most impressive sights of a Roman morning may be seen every weekday from eight to nine in all the streets which converge upon the Piazza della Pilotta. Every turning pours out its quota of young men, all in their twenties, wearing a great variety of ecclesiastical costume, or rather many versions of the same costume. Most of them carry brief cases and books, and all of them wear, especially at examination time, an anxious, strained expression which is common to students everywhere. They approach the portals of a building which bears the words upon it PONTIFICIA UNIVERSI-TAS GREGORIANA, and is known to all those young men as "the Gregorian," or simply as "the Greg." It is the Oxford-Cambridge-Yale-Harvard of the Church.

The young scholars come from the various seminaries which are scattered all over Rome. They are of almost every nationality, and one glances at them with speculative interest and curiosity. Some no doubt will remain village priests all their lives, a few may perhaps achieve a diocese, one or two possibly a red hat—and—is it possible?—is there a future Pope among them? There well may be. Among students of the Gregorian were Gregory XV, Urban VIII, Innocent X, Clement IX, Innocent XII, Clement XI, Innocent XIII, Clement XII, Leo XIII and the late Pope, Pius XII.

What strikes me about the students is that, unlike any similar group of young men at an ordinary university, they all tend to look alike; indeed the uniformity is astonishing. It is true that the dress they wear does not admit of any eccentricity or expression of individuality, but there is more to it than that. Each student, from no matter what part of the world he has come, has been selected by his bishop for the same reason: that he has a vocation for the priesthood. After a year or two in Rome the discipline of the Church puts its stamp upon the young men as clearly as the army upon its soldiers. The difference is, of course, that the army's discipline is external while the discipline of the Church is also of the mind and the spirit.

Students leaving the Gregorian, seen from a window of the Biblicum

It is interesting to watch the seminarists as they ascend the steps of their university and to tell their nationality from their dress. The older colleges wear a long black or colored cassock and belt, with a sleeveless coat called the *soprana* from whose armholes hang two long strings. One has often heard of someone "in leading strings," and here is the real thing. The "leading strings" of the *soprana* symbolize a state of tuition or dependence. They are also to be seen hanging from the armholes of the Pope's *camerieri di cappa e spada*. The English students wear a black cassock and *soprana* without a sash, the Scots wear a purple cassock with crimson sash, buttons and pipings and a black *soprana*; the Irish wear a black cassock with red pipings, no sash and a black *soprana*; the North Americans wear a double-breasted black cassock, blue piping and buttons and a crimson sash; the South Americans wear a black cassock with blue edgings and a blue sash. There are many more variations of the same style of dress and with a little study the visitor can spot the nationality of a seminarist at a glance. The most spectacular, and known to everyone, are the Germans, who wear cardinal red with a black sash. They give to the streets of Rome something of that color given to London by the Brigade of Guards. During the last war it was considered prudent for the German seminarists to go into black, but immediately the war was over, the Romans clamored for the return of the red cassocks and were not satisfied until these appeared on the streets again.

The reason for this spectacular costume—more spectacular than any except that of a cardinal—is not exactly known. One unkind story, which is popular with students of other nationalities, is that the Germans were put into red in order that they might be easily detected if they entered beer halls! A more charitable explanation is that St. Ignatius of Loyola, who founded the German College, gave them the red cassocks to remind them that when they became priests and returned to Protestant Germany of the sixteenth century, they might have to shed their blood for their faith. The Roman nickname for the German seminarists is *gamberi*, which means crabs.

101

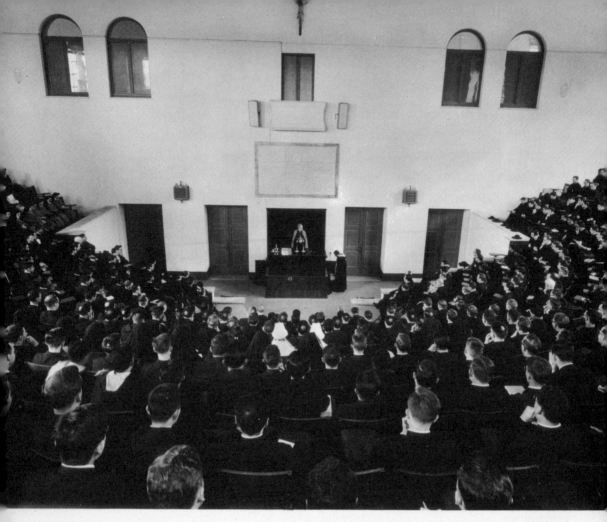

Lecture at the College of the Congregation
for the Propagation of the Faith

Two thousand five hundred young men may be seen entering
the Gregorian University every day and they come from more than
two hundred colleges and religious orders. The teaching staff numbers a hundred and ten professors, and all lectures are in Latin. The
undergraduate course is three years for Philosophy and four years
for Theology. It is amusing to watch the young priests-to-be come
pouring out into the piazza during the morning "break," when they
mill around in groups just like any other crowd of undergraduates
as they speak to one another in Italian or dog Latin. It is obvious
that a cassock and a priest's hat do not extinguish a sense of fun or

dampen the high spirits of youth. I smiled to watch a group of students joking with one of their class, a young Trinitarian, who was wearing sandals, a white habit and a black cloak bearing a blue and red cross upon it. As they joked, one of the seminarists twirled the rope that girded the waist of the young Trinitarian and administered one or two by-no-means-gentle taps with the end of it.

Facing the University is an institution known as "the Biblicum," whose full name is The Pontifical Biblical Institute, which celebrated its jubilee in 1959. It is housed in an old palace whose courtyard possesses one of the most beautiful of Rome's private and unknown fountains. The Biblical Institute exists to train professors of Scripture, Biblical interpretation, and scientific research. There are two faculties, one for Biblical study and the other for the study of the languages and literature of the ancient East. One of the professors remarked to me, as we were discussing the importance of the Dead Sea Scrolls: "There are two studies which are making most progress today. One is the study of atomic physics and the other the study of the ancient Near East."

Seminarians from all nations with the lecturer

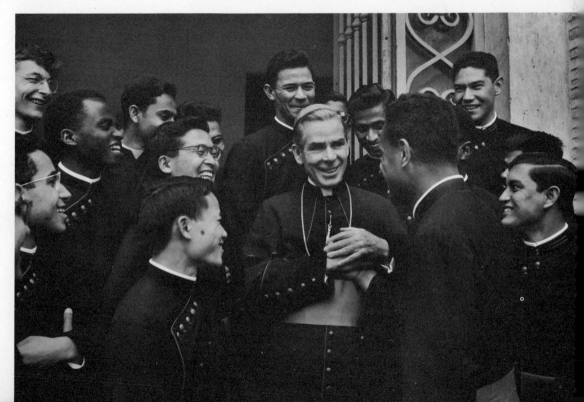

A ROMAN KEYHOLE

As you explore the Aventine Hill you may come upon a small piazza designed by Piranesi and bearing a strong resemblance to one of his etchings. It is a quiet, secluded corner of Rome and might be even more tranquil were it not for a keyhole in an ancient gateway. Though it is called a "keyhole" in all the books it is really a small circular hole cut in the wood of the gate immediately above the real keyhole.

Coaches arrive in this tranquil square all day, while tourists apply their eyes to the "keyhole," and are always delighted with what they see. This is a garden path lying between two dark laurel hedges which converge to a point where, perfectly framed and far off on the opposite bank of the Tiber, is seen the dome of St. Peter's. It is a magic and unexpected glimpse. Surely there is something amusing—almost impertinent—in the use of Michelangelo's mighty dome as a peepshow!

The gateway is that of the Villa of the Priory of the Knights of Malta, whose arms are sculptured above it. Inside, entering an old garden, one walks, admiring the shrubberies, the flower beds, an old fountain, and a summer house decorated from floor to ceiling with the arms of Grand Masters of the Order, a museum of international heraldry.

Sometimes elderly Italian noblemen may be seen walking together in the garden. They are the modern representatives of the Sovereign Order of the Knights Hospitallers of St. John, afterwards known as the Knights of Rhodes, and, later, as the Knights of Malta, the oldest of all the semi-monastic orders of Chivalry. Their history is one of devotion to the Christian faith, and of compassion for the

Looking through the keyhole at the Villa of the Knights of Malta

sick and unfortunate; it is also a history of spectacular but stubborn retreat, first from the Holy Land, then from Cyprus, Rhodes, and eventually Malta. For two centuries the Knights, as a naval power, kept the infidel out of Europe, and it was in one of their galleys that Pope Gregory XI returned to Rome from Avignon in 1377.

Travelers in the Middle Ages thought the hospital of the Knights one of the wonders of the world. A sick man was given the Sacrament and was carried to his bed "as if the Knights were carrying the Master and Head of all." The world had to wait many a long century before such medical skill and nursing were to be known again, and even today no hospital serves its patients on gold plate as the Knights did in the days of their magnificence!

Since the retreat from Rhodes in 1522 and from Malta in 1798 (where the name of Valetta commemorates the Grand Master, Lavalette) the history of the Order has been one of reorganization and revival in many parts of the world as nursing and ambulance associations. In 1888 Queen Victoria restored the Order by Royal Charter in England, and her son, afterwards King Edward VII, became the first Grand Prior since Tudor times.

In Rome the Knights still cling to the shadow of their former power and maintain diplomatic relations with twenty-five foreign countries. There are eleven associations of the Knights of St. John in Europe and twelve in the Americas, including two in the United States and one in Canada. The main charitable activities have not changed with the times or with the altered fortunes of the Order: care of the sick, of lepers, of wounded in war and peace, of refugees, and medical assistance to Catholic missions.

At the end of the "Garden of the Keyhole" is the Priory church where the banners of the different language groups—the famous *Langues*—into which the Order was divided, hang in the nave. These banners are of Aragon, England, Castile, France, Italy, and Germany. The flags are the ancient blazons and would not be readily recognized today except by heralds; for instance, the English

The "keyhole view," Villa of the Knights of Malta

flag is that of the Plantagenets—the lilies of France quartered with the leopards of England.

As the visitor to Rome looks through the peephole in the gate, he may think how strange it is that the thunders of the Crusades should have died away to a garden path between a laurel hedge. But he should also remember that the Order is still alive, and still dispensing charity and help to the suffering. One might call it the most ancient good deed in the world.

The Swiss Guard on parade

THE SWISS GUARD

WE WENT to St. Peter's one morning at that lovely hour, soon after six, before the mad Roman traffic has begun its new noisy day, when the little squares are deserted and you can actually hear the voices of the smallest fountains. The vast piazza was empty, half in sun, half in shadow; and we went to the Gate of St. Ann, where a Swiss Guard admitted us into the Vatican City.

We had come to see recruits to the Swiss Guard take their oath of fidelity to the Pope, a picturesque ceremony which occurs once a year. The sun, just riding above the curving arm of Bernini's colonnade, was spilling over into the old fortresslike buildings which crowd together beneath the Vatican Palace. The ceremony was to take place in an oddly shaped courtyard, formed by the outer curve of the arm of the colonnade with that angle of the palace which contains the papal apartments.

There was a rap of kettledrums as one of the most colorful processions that even Rome can provide emerged from an ancient gateway and formed in the courtyard. Led by two drummers with silver kettledrums slanted in front of them, and followed by four Swiss Guards playing fifes, came the whole corps, two by two, like a number of tropical wasps or dragonflies, as they passed from shadow into splashes of early sunlight. Each man, striped from neck to gaitered feet in bands of vivid red, yellow, and blue, wore a starched white ruff at his throat and upon his head a steel casque, from which rose a dark red plume. Each one carried an eight-foot halberd with a damascened head. The officers might have stepped from a canvas by Velásquez. They wore doublets with slashed sleeves and breeches of mulberry-colored velvet. Their stockings were of the same color

110

and they wore buckled shoes. The plumes in their steel helmets were red, except for the commandant who wore the only white plume on parade. From each left hip slanted a thin rapier with a steel pommel.

A guard of honor with the flag formed up in the center of the line. The flag, really a large banner, bears the tiara and the crossed keys on a red ground in one quarter, while the other three are stripes of red, yellow, and blue divided by a white cross, in the center of which, within a green wreath, are the arms of the reigning Pope.

The sergeant major, facing the colors, read the oath of allegiance to the Pope. Then one by one, the names of the recruits were called out. As each man heard his name, he sprang to attention, handed his halberd to the man next to him, and, taking a step forward, executed a smart right or left turn and marched to the colors, which at his approach was lowered to waist level. Grasping the shaft of the flag with a left hand in a white cotton glove, and with a right white-cottoned hand held into the air, the recruit shouted in a loud, dramatic voice, which probably carried as far as the Holy Father's apartments immediately above.

"I swear," he shouted, "to observe loyally and in good faith all that has been read to me at this moment. May God and His saints help me!"

He then returned to his place in the ranks. Those from the German-speaking cantons took the oath in German, those from the French-speaking, in French. All the men came from the four Catholic cantons of Unterwalden, Lucerne, Uri, and Schwyz. They must be Catholics, bachelors, between eighteen and twenty-five years of age and at least five feet eleven inches in height. After ten years of service they receive a pension. As one rarely sees an elderly Swiss Guard, it is obvious that its members retire at an early age. Service in the corps is almost a hereditary occupation, and the same names occur in the records century after century.

Like the Varangian Guard, which protected the Byzantine Emperors, and probably all foreign bodyguards in history, the Swiss

Guard remains a small foreign colony during their service in Rome and have little to do with the Italians. Few of them speak more than a few elementary words of the language. They eat in their own Swiss canteen food cooked by Swiss cooks, and they drink, not the wine of Italy, but their own beer. And on their days off these guardians of the Holy Father wander out to see the sights of Rome, undistinguishable from any other young Swiss tourists in Rome.

The mind refuses to grapple with such mathematical problems as the film mileage expended upon them in the course of a year. They are the most photographed soldiers in the world.

Dome of St. Peter's and Vatican Radio tower
from the Vatican Gardens

Papal coat of arms, Palace of the Governor, Vatican City

There was a tap on a drum. The parade came to attention. One saw them disappear kaleidoscopically beneath the archway with the thought that Rome had kept another delightful appointment with her past.

THE VATICAN GARDENS

THE Vatican Gardens were often unapproachable in the afternoon during the reign of Pius XII, when the Pope was in Rome. His Holiness liked to pace up and down the covered walk in the gardens, rarely lifting his eyes from the pages of a book, attended only by the chamberlain on duty and the commander of the Noble Guards. During this time even the police effaced themselves, for the Holy Father liked to enjoy the illusion that he was alone and unobserved.

Nowadays the atmosphere in the Gardens is quite informal and friendly. A gardener, bedding out the papal coat-of-arms in front of the governor's palace, would not now be surprised to be greeted by the Pope John and to be asked how much he earns a week.

From 1870 until the signing of the Lateran Treaty in 1929 the Vatican Gardens were the only territory in which "the prisoner of the Vatican" could take a walk, and naturally successive Popes have shown interest in gardening, in the laying-out of flower beds, in fountains, and even in the keeping of tame animals. That the Vatican lawns are among the few in Rome to remain green all through the summer is due entirely to Pius XI, who constructed two new reservoirs and arranged the most modern type of irrigation in all parts of the gardens.

In the old days perhaps the most interesting feature of the Gardens was the Papal Observatory, but this no longer exists. It has

114

Toe of statue of St. Peter, St. Pete

been removed to Castel Gandolfo. Today the most important feature is Vatican Radio, a scene of round-the-clock activity. This up-to-date station is manned by the Jesuits, and broadcasts are given in nearly every language, including Chinese, Russian, Slovene, and Albanian. So far, there is no Vatican television.

One of the chief glories of the Vatican Gardens is the view of the Dome of St. Peter's, which from this viewpoint is seen just as its architect would have wished.

ST. PETER'S TOE

THE bronze St. Peter is enthroned in the nave of his basilica, upright in a chair, a halo upon his head, one hand lifted in benediction, the other holding the Keys of Heaven. The right leg is advanced so that half his foot protrudes beyond the edge of the plinth. His manner is Roman and magisterial. The tradition is that the statue was made by order of Leo I, about A.D. 440 as a thanksgiving for Rome's delivery from Attila.

Pilgrims come forward all day long and perform the ancient homage of kissing his foot. The little gold crosses embroidered upon the Pope's red shoes today are a relic of this custom, and a sign that the reverence was paid not to him but to the Son of God.

The right foot of the statue is as smooth as brown glass and the shape of the toes has been obliterated by centuries of kissing. This is an extremely moving sight. In places the bronze shines like brass, and the right toes, which are so clearly defined in the unkissed left foot, are now deformed and resemble a shoe.

It is interesting to see how pilgrims kiss the toe. We watched while some fifty men and women did so one morning and each one, without exception, before kissing it, smoothed it with a hand in a

116

swift caressing way as if wiping off the last kiss before implanting a new one. But I am sure there was nothing antiseptic about this gesture. It was a desire to touch a revered object and to draw near physically to the odor of sanctity. It may be that the toe of St. Peter has been worn away as much by hands as by lips.

One comes out of the east end of St. Peter's into a blaze of morning sun that shines full upon the façade of the building. This is contrary to established custom, but Constantine built all his churches

Plaza of St. Peter's

to face the rising sun. A great part of the wonder and delight experienced in the morning, as one sees St. Peter's with its grand flight of steps, its monumental façade with Corinthian pilasters and semi-pilasters crowned by white statues of our Lord and the Apostles, is due to this orientation. For sixteen centuries pilgrims have enjoyed the morning light upon St. Peter's, first upon the Byzantine basilica and now upon the probably less beautiful but more splendid and monumental church. Was this system or orientation, which was seen also in the ancient Lateran, the first St. Paul's, St. Lawrence, the Church of the Holy Sepulchre, in Jerusalem—the *Anastasis*—and the churches in Tyre and Antioch, a fancy of the Emperor's? It was also the orientation of the pagan temples; that may be one of the reasons why the Church so quickly reversed it and made the apse face the East.

THE POPE IN ST. PETER'S

ST. PETER'S is crowded to the doors. At any moment the trumpets will sound to announce the arrival of the Pope, who is to assist at Benediction and to revere the relics of a beatified Canadian nun, the Blessed Margaret d'Youville.

At the extreme end of the church, in the Tribune, six young members of the Canadian College, holding tall candles, face each other on either side of an altar beneath Bernini's fantastic *Cathedra Petri*. Canadian bishops take their places behind the cardinals, and farther back in a tribune sit tier upon tier, and row after row, of "Grey Sisters," who have come from Canada to be present at the beatification of the foundress of their Order, the Sisters of Charity of Montreal. Their eager, excited faces glance this way and that, and their eyes miss nothing.

118

The wait in St. Peter's before a papal ceremony is like nothing else in the world. An hour passes as if it were five minutes. There is always something to see: a cardinal passing to his place to a rustle of scarlet silk; the Diplomatic Corps in uniform with plumed hats and swords; their ladies in black with mantillas; the Swiss Guard; the papal gendarmerie; the eager crowd itself pressing into the church until it seems that St. Peter's cannot possibly hold one more human being. Suddenly and unexpectedly hundreds of crystal chandeliers all over the church sparkle into light, and an "oh!" of delight and expectancy whispers through the building. The Holy Father is about to appear! The six young Canadian students holding candles glance at each other with some trepidation. It must be a strange experience to be taken out of the classroom by the Blessed Margaret d'Youville and placed in the most prominent position in a papal ceremony!

Silver trumpets ring through the basilica. The choir sings *Tu es Petrus*, then the band plays the Pontifical March by Silveri; and far away at the end of the nave rises wave after wave of cheering in which it is possible to detect the cry *"Viva il Papa!"* The Pope is being carried into St. Peter's. Still those near the Tribune can see nothing: their view down the church is obstructed by Bernini's Baldachino. The cheering grows nearer as the papal procession approaches, and now it is possible to see, moving through the crowd, the plumed steel helmets of the Swiss Guard, a line of advancing halberds, the brass helmets of the Noble Guard; a chamberlain with an El Greco face and beard, with a ruff about his neck; then, high above the crowd so that everyone can see, the most astonishing and awe-inspiring of all ceremonial spectacles: the Pope in white seated in the *sedia gestatoria*, carried forward slowly upon the shoulders of the bearers, tracing in the air, with uplifted hand to right and to left, the sign of the Cross.

No royal sovereign has ever achieved such an effect as the entry of this Priest in white; for the eye and the mind of the spectator are fired at the same moment, and one sees not one Pope but the last

119

Beatification of blessed Margaret d'Youville, St. Peter's

Pope in an unbroken chain of Popes stretching back into the mists of Time, beyond the Renaissance into the Middle Ages, and still back into the Dark Ages, to the Catacombs, to Imperial Rome itself —to St. Peter. When the Pope enters St. Peter's, the gates of Time are flung wide open and one hears a Voice . . . *"Tu es Petrus et super hanc petram ædificabo ecclesiam meam et tibi dabo claves regni caelorum."*[1]

I reflect that I have seen three Popes carried in state into St. Peter's. I saw Pius XI borne in upon a wave of cheering such as I never conceived possible, when he celebrated Pontifical High Mass after the signing of the Lateran Treaty in 1929; I saw Pius XII on many occasions, thin, aristocratic, carrying his honors easily like an aged Augustus, his almost transparent hand tracing the Cross in the air, his face expressionless, frozen in calm, his effect upon one that

[1] Thou art Peter, and it is upon this rock that I will build my church . . . And I will give to thee the keys of the kingdom of heaven.   MATTHEW XVI: 18, 19

His Holiness, Pope John XXIII, at the beatification
of blessed Margaret d'Youville

of a visible holiness; and now comes John XXIII to the sound of the same trumpets, the same tramp upon marble, the same *"Vivas!"*

While I feel that Pius XII was the most exquisite Pope it would be possible to see, I also have the feeling that John XXIII is probably the most human pontiff within living memory; and I think what a complete contrast he is—a Vespasian rather than an Augustus—to his predecessor. The Romans already feel for him something of that affection which still clings to the memory of *Pio Nono*.

In his reign so far John XXIII has filled the world with stories of what Kipling called "the common touch," which really means Christian kindness and humanity. Only a man of extraordinary force of character could have projected his personality through the apparently impenetrable screen of Vatican protocol and etiquette; but he has done so until there can scarcely be anyone who has not heard some kind story about him. It is well known that he invited a poor priest to share his Christmas dinner; that he explores the Vatican, talking to humble servants of their financial and family problems; that he ordered a dinner to be given to men in prison. But it is not so well known, perhaps, that he also insisted that this meal should be served by nuns, so that men removed by their deeds from the softer influences in life should see the hands of women ministering to them; and I am told by one who was present that nothing affected the prisoners so much as the knowledge that the Pope had withdrawn their warders and had thought them worthy to be served by women vowed to Christ.

The bearers lower the *sedia gestatoria*, and the Pope, stepping down, is conducted to a faldstool facing the altar. He is vested in a rich cope and kneels in prayer while the rite of Benediction proceeds. A priest, wearing a humeral veil, advances to the altar with two assistants and opens the tabernacle, exposing the Host and placing it in a monstrance. As two verses of the hymn, *Pange lingua*, are sung, beginning *Tantum ergo sacramentum* . . . the Pope is conducted to the altar where, after incensing the Blessed Sacrament, he

122

The Tomb of Pope Pius XII, St. Peter's

returns to his faldstool. The officiating Prelate (in this case Cardinal Léger of Montreal) who wears a cope and puts on over it a humeral veil (always used when carrying the host) gives the blessing.

Then the relics of the new *beata*, the Blessed Margaret d'Youville, are brought to the Pope in a wooden chest. He prays over them and venerates them, after which one of those charming little scenes occur which one fancies survive from other times. A member of the papal household appears unexpectedly in the Tribune holding a bouquet of flowers for the Holy Father. But it is unlike any bouquet known to a modern florist; it is a cone-shaped object about four feet in height, not unlike a Christmas tree, covered with roses.

The Pope is now conducted to the *sedia gestatoria*, the procession forms up again, the bouquet is carried by a monsignor, the trumpets sound once more; and the figure in white above the heads of the cheering multitude, tracing a blessing in the air glides slowly. . . .

On the Feast of Pentecost the Pope attended Vespers in St. Peter's. Such an event had not been known since the reign of Leo XIII, and hardly anyone in the church guessed what a beautiful and unusual tradition was to be revived.

Bernini colonnade, St. Peter's

It was the custom in ancient times to symbolize in a variety of ways, some of them rather thoughtlessly cruel to our own ideas, the descent of the Holy Spirit upon the disciples in the form of Pentecostal flames. For instance, in the Middle Ages doves were let loose in St. Peter's, and large numbers of small birds were released with streamers of red wool tied to their legs, representing tongues of fire. At one time an even more realistic custom was to drop burning tow upon the Pope's head as he moved in procession down the church. This, of course, burst into brief puffs of fire round him and, though perhaps rather disconcerting to the pontiff, must have been extremely effective to the onlookers. But the most beautiful of all Pentecostal symbolism appears to have originated in the Pantheon,

where the large central opening in the roof inspired the idea of casting red rose-petals into the church. It may be, of course, that the venerable custom of showering white rose-petals during High Mass in St. Mary Major on August 5th (which still takes place in the Borghese Chapel), was the actual inspiration, though the aperture in the roof of the Pantheon must certainly have encouraged it and have helped in its execution. At any rate, the white rose-petals of St. Mary Major, which symbolize the miraculous fall of snow in August, A.D. 352, when the church was founded, were succeeded during the Feast of Pentecost by red rose-petals in the Pantheon—and later in St. Peter's—symbolizing tongues of fire.

Therefore when John XXIII attended Vespers on Sunday, May 17, 1959, a surprised and puzzled congregation noticed something fluttering down from the dome upon the high altar. It was a little time before it was realized that these drifting objects were red rose-petals, and only a few knew that they symbolized the Pentecostal fire and that St. Peter's was witnessing a sight unknown in this century.

The task of showering rose-petals upon the high altar was entrusted to a member of the Sanpietrini, the corps of workmen who keep the fabric of St. Peter's in repair. It was not as simple as it might appear. To let them drift down from the gallery of the dome would not have been effective, for they would have fallen unevenly and to one side or the other. They had to be showered from the highest, and most central, point of the dome, the Lantern, 405 feet above the floor of the church. Unfortunately no record existed of the amount of rose-petals necessary to cover the high altar of St. Peter's, and the result was that the fall was not quite as heavy as it was intended to be. But next time twice as many rose-petals will be carried to the Lantern.

TWO SAINTS RETURN TO ROME

G IUSEPPE MELCHIORRE SARTO was born in the year 1835 in the village of Riese, in the northern part of Venezia, the son of humble parents. He became Cardinal and Patriarch of Venice in 1893; he was elected Pope, as Pius X, in 1903, and, after a pontificate of eleven years, he died in 1914 and was canonized in 1954.

In 1959 fifty-six years had passed since that day when the future Pope bade farewell to Venice in order to attend the conclave and promised his friends—for he had no idea that he might be elected Pope—that he would one day return. This he was fated never to do. Never again was he to see his beloved province, whose musical dialect he loved to speak; never again was he to see the eternally magic city of canals and bridges, where the basilica of St. Mark's stands glittering like a box of jewels upon one of the world's finest squares. Instead, this son of Venetian peasant stock was to shoulder what he regarded as the heaviest of all life's burdens: the Papacy.

In 1959 another Patriarch of Venice occupied the throne of St. Peter, John XXIII. Remembering how deeply his saintly predecessor had loved his native land, and his unfulfilled promise to return there, Pope John ordered that the body of St. Pius X should be taken to Venice and exposed for veneration in St. Mark's. The voyage in state up the Grand Canal, and the lying in state before the high altar in St. Mark's, were among the most impressive events of the year 1959.

On the day that the body of St. Pius X returned to Rome, together with the body of St. John Bosco, we received permission from the Vatican authorities to witness the ceremony from the southern arm of Bernini's Colonnade. Just as the sun was setting we met a

127

Following pages: The reception of the bodies of St. John Bosco and St. Pius X, St. Peter's

His Holiness, Pope John XXIII

member of the Sanpietrini who, after unlocking gates and doors, led the way up a flight of dark stone steps which ended on the top of the colonnade.

Thousands pass beneath Bernini's Colonnade every year, but few have ever stood on top of it. Here, in the center of Rome, is an unknown world, a great circle of stone occupied by enormous saints whose statues tower up everywhere, immense and distorted to suit the vision of those who see them from below. We were fascinated to find the colonnade roofed with eighteenth-century red tiles invisible from the piazza, and that it is possible to walk the length of it under cover. Most remarkable of all, so it seemed to us, was that, like the Colosseum in the eighteenth to nineteenth centuries, Bernini's Colonnade possesses its own flourishing vegetation. Blown by the wind, or carried up there by birds, are hundreds of little rock plants and grasses lodged in cracks in the masonry, so many that a botanist could probably write a fascinating paper on the flora of that untrodden island of stone in the heart of Rome. We looked in amazement at several fig trees, three and four feet in height, which flourished apparently in a few grains of sand and dust blown up from the piazza by the winds of spring and winter.

Glancing between the stone balusters, we saw, far below, the twin plumes of the fountains, the obelisk in the square and, to the west, the mighty façade of St. Peter's, upon whose steps a portable altar had been erected. Cardinals, members of the diplomatic Corps, and other dignitaries were grouped on either side. As it grew dark we heard the sound of drums and trumpets from the Vatican, and through a lane of spectators came the Noble and Swiss Guard, behind them men with lanterns escorting the Pope on the *sedia gestatoria*.

Then from the Via della Conciliazione came the sound of chanting and, looking down, we saw a great company of priests and monks with processional crosses and banners advancing in front of two hearses, each one drawn by four plumed horses. Upon these hearses lay the glass coffins in which the bodies of St. Pius X and St. John Bosco were clearly visible.

The coffins were placed upon the portable altar. The Pope left his throne and, ascending the steps of St. Peter's to the altar, knelt there in prayer for a long time. Then the drums and trumpets sounded again and, taking his seat on the *sedia gestatoria*, John XXIII was borne into the Vatican Palace.

We stumbled down the stone stairway in the dark, feeling rather like explorers who had returned to the world.

"MY NAME IS JOHN"

THE fortunate boy, who was standing upon the Appian Way when this book began, ended his pilgrimage to Rome with a private audience with the Pope. His Holiness asked the boy's name, and, upon hearing that it was Jerome, he spoke to him about the saint, then said with a smile:

"My name is John and my father's name was John. Of course, God always knew that I should be a Pope some day, and though He has had more than seventy years to work on me, isn't it strange that He hasn't made me nicer to look at?"

In those few words the Holy Father expressed those qualities which have endeared him to so many: humor, humility, and just a gentle touch of irony.

Leaving the Vatican through the Gates of Bronze after the Papal audience

Throwing a coin into the Fountain of Trevi

In the morning young Jerome threw his coin into the Fontana di Trevi and said good-bye to Rome. He had seen the Seven Churches; he had seen many of the *tituli;* he had spoken to the Holy Father. He had done the things that pilgrims have done since the earliest ages, that would-be pilgrims hope to do when their turn comes to see the Eternal City.

Back at school with a prized souvenir

ABOUT THIS BOOK

AND THE MEN WHO MADE IT

Mr. Morton, Bishop Sheen, Mr. Karsh (*left to right*)

FULTON JOHN SHEEN was born May 8, 1895, at El Paso, Illinois, one of four sons of Newton Morris and Delia (Fulton) Sheen. He was baptized Peter and took the name John at confirmation, later adopting his mother's maiden name. His father was a farmer, but the family later moved to Peoria, Ill., where he attended St. Mary's School and Spalding Institute from which he was graduated in 1913. He received his A.B. and M.A. degrees from St. Viator College, Bourbonnais, Ill., where he first tasted the pleasures of speaking and writing as a member of the college debating team and newspaper staff. He completed his theological studies at St. Paul's Seminary, St. Paul, Minn., and was ordained to the priesthood for the Diocese of Peoria, September 20, 1919. A year later he obtained his degrees of Bachelor of Sacred Theology and Bachelor of Canon Law from the Catholic University of America, and went to the University of Louvain, Belgium, where he was awarded a Ph.D. in 1923. He also attended the Sorbonne in Paris and the Collegio Angelico in Rome. In 1924 he received his Doctorate of Sacred Theology in Rome, and a year later while teaching dogmatic theology at St. Edmund's College, Ware, England, he was made an Agrégé en Philosophie by Louvain and awarded that university's Cardinal Mercier International Philosophy Award. His honorary degrees include LL.D., Litt.D. and L.H.D. On his return to the United States, he served as a curate of St. Patrick's Church in Peoria and joined the faculty of the Catholic University of America, Washington, D.C., in 1926 as a philosophy of religion instructor, later being promoted to a full professorship. In June, 1934, he was appointed Papal Chamberlain and was elevated the following year to Domestic Prelate. He was conse-

139

crated Bishop on June 11, 1951, a year after he became National Director of the Society for the Propagation of the Faith. As a preacher he has been heard by millions in the United States, Canada and England, through the media of radio and television. A prolific writer, he is author of two syndicated columns: "God Love You" for the Catholic press, and "Bishop Sheen Speaks," for the secular press; and is editor of two magazines: World-mission, a quarterly review, and Mission, a bimonthly. The popularity of his radio and television programs can be judged from the fact that his daily mail as a result of these programs has reached as much as ten thousand letters in a single day—about one-third of them from non-Catholics. The largest single delivery of mail after a program was thirty thousand letters. He conducted the first religious service ever telecast, served as narrator for a March of Time film, and has had his sermons issued in record album form. His interests are wide and as well as serving in such organizations as the Catholic Literary Guild and the American Catholic Philosophical Society, he is an active member of the Mediaeval Academy and the American Geographical Association. The long list of his books started with publication of *God and Intelligence in Modern Philosophy* (Longmans, Green, 1925). This was followed by *Religion Without God* (Longmans, Green, 1928), *The Life of All Living* (Century, 1929), *The Divine Romance* (Century, 1930), *Old Errors and New Labels* (Century, 1931), *Moods and Truths* (Century, 1932), *The Way of the Cross* (Appleton-Century, 1933), *Seven Last Words* (Appleton-Century, 1933), *The Eternal Galilean* (Appleton-Century, 1934), *The Philosophy of Science* (Bruce, 1934), *The Mystical Body of Christ* (Sheed and Ward, 1935), *Calvary and the Mass* (Kenedy, 1936), *The Moral Universe* (Bruce, 1936), *The Cross and the Beatitudes* (Kenedy, 1937), *The Cross and the Crisis* (Bruce, 1938), *Liberty, Equality and Fraternity* (Macmillan, 1938), *The Rainbow of Sorrow* (Kenedy, 1938), *Victory Over Vice* (Kenedy, 1939), *Freedom Under God* (Bruce, 1940), *Whence Come Wars* (Sheed and Ward, 1940), *The Seven Virtues* (Kenedy, 1940), *For God and Country* (Kenedy, 1941), *A Declaration of Dependence* (Bruce, 1941), *God and War* (Kenedy, 1942), *The Divine Verdict* (Kenedy, 1943), *The Armor of God* (Kenedy, 1943), *Philosophies at War* (Scribner's, 1943), *Seven Words to the Cross* (Kenedy, 1944), *Seven Pillars of Peace* (Scribner's, 1944), *Love One Another* (Kenedy, 1944), *Seven Words of Jesus and Mary* (Kenedy, 1945), *Preface to Religion* (Kenedy, 1946), *Characters of the Passion* (Kenedy, 1946), *Jesus, Son of Mary* (McMullen, 1947), *Communism and the Conscience of the West* (Bobbs, Merrill, 1948), *Philosophy of Religion* (Appleton-Century-Crofts, 1948), *Peace of Soul* (McGraw-Hill, 1949), *Lift Up Your Heart* (McGraw-Hill, 1950), *Three to Get Married* (Appleton-Century-Crofts, 1951), *The World's First Love* (McGraw-Hill, 1952), *Life Is Worth Living, First Series* (McGraw-Hill, 1953), *Life Is Worth Living, Second Series* (McGraw-Hill, 1954), *The Life of Christ* (McGraw-Hill, 1954), *The Way to*

140

Happiness (Garden City, 1954), *Life Is Worth Living, Third Series* (Mc-Graw-Hill, 1955), *The Way to Inner Peace* (Garden City, 1955), *God Love You* (Garden City, 1955), *Thinking Life Through* (Garden City, 1955), *The True Meaning of Christmas* (McGraw-Hill, 1955), *Life Is Worth Living, Fourth Series* (Mc-Graw-Hill, 1956), *Thoughts for Daily Living* (Garden City, 1956), *Life Is Worth Living, Fifth Series* (Mc-Graw-Hill, 1957), *This Is the Mass* (Hawthorn, 1958). He is Auxiliary Bishop of New York.

YOUSUF KARSH was born December 23, 1908, at Mardin, Armenia, and left for Canada at the age of fifteen during the Turkish massacres. Son of an import-export entrepreneur and grandson of an engraver, he went to stay with an uncle, A. G. Nakash, who owned a photography studio in Sherbrooke, Quebec. He took an interest in the art of the camera and was sent by his uncle to Boston to study. After several years in the United States he went to open his own studio in Canada's capital, where within a few years he was photographing the cream of society and leaders of government. When war broke out in 1939, Ottawa became a center of Allied war activity and "Karsh of Ottawa" became a familiar signature on the portraits of some of the world's greatest leaders. His famous portrait of Winston Churchill in 1941 rocketed him to fame as the world's greatest portrait photographer, and that photograph along with seventy-four others, taken in all parts of the world in the four years that followed, went into making his first book, *Faces of Destiny* (Ziff-Davis, 1946). He followed this with *This Is the Mass* (Hawthorn, 1958) and *Portraits of Greatness* (Thomas Nelson & Sons, 1959). Still a world traveler, he keeps cameras and equipment at studios in London, Paris and New York, as well as in Ottawa, and usually carries a set of traveling equipment that weighs a minimum of 250 pounds. He always uses a white camera, finding that the traditional black is too depressing, and his focusing cloth varies in color with his own mood—though it is most often of red velvet with a gold satin lining. Groups of his portraits form part of the permanent collections of such museums as the Brooklyn Museum Department of Photography and the Museum of Modern Art in New York, Eastman House, Rochester, N.Y., The Art Institute of Chicago, and the Huntington Library, San Marino, Cal. In acknowledgment of his contribution to Canadian art and culture he received one of the first Canadian Citizenship Certificates in January, 1947, when Parliament passed a law creating Canadian citizenship. He is actively interested in Canadian theatre and met Solange Gauthier, whom he married in 1939, when she was acting with the Ottawa Drama League. She serves frequently as model for his work and shares his love for gardening and tennis.

H. V. Morton, author and traveler, was born in England in 1892. He has been called the "world's greatest travel writer." At the age of nineteen he became Assistant Editor on the Birmingham *Gazette and Express*. He then went to the London *Daily Mail* where he stayed until the outbreak of World War I. After four years in the Royal Army he returned to England and began to explore the British Isles. He started with a study of England and its people which was published as *In Search of England*. Then came Scotland in *In Search of Scotland*. *In Search of Ireland* gave the flavor of the Emerald Isle. He became an honorary "bard" for *In Search of Wales*. Mr. Morton next turned his attention to the land where Christianity first began. *In the Steps of the Master* recounted a trip that followed the journeyings of Jesus in the Holy Land. He next followed the path of the three missionary journeys of the Apostle Paul in his *In the Steps of St. Paul*. His masterpiece of biblical history, *The Lands of the Bible,* was a travel narrative of a trip through all the ancient lands mentioned in the Bible—Babylon, Egypt, the Holy Land, the sites of the ancient kingdoms and empires in the time of biblical events. Going on to new adventures, he is now writing of European countries and has completed books on Spain and Italy. He is the author of *The Heart of London* (1925), *London* (1926), *The London Year* (1926), *The Spell of London* (1926), *The Nights of London* (1926), *In Search of England* (Dodd, Mead, 1927), *The Call of England* (Dodd, Mead, 1928), *In Search of Scotland* (Dodd, Mead, 1930), *In Search of Ireland* (Dodd, Mead, 1931), *In Search of Wales* (Dodd, Mead, 1932), *Blue Days at Sea* (Dodd, Mead, 1932), *In Scotland Again* (Dodd Mead, 1933), *In the Steps of the Master* (Dodd, Mead, 1934), *The London Scene* (Dodd, Mead, 1935), *Our Fellow Men* (Dodd, Mead, 1936), *In the Steps of St. Paul* (Dodd, Mead, 1936), *The Lands of the Bible* (Dodd, Mead, 1938), *Ghosts of London* (Dodd, Mead, 1939), *In Search of the Northern Isles* (1940), *Women of the Bible* (1940), *Middle East* (1941), *I, James Blunt* (1942), *Morton's London* (Dodd, Mead, 1950), *Stranger in Spain* (Dodd, Mead, 1954), *Traveller in Rome* (Dodd, Mead, 1957). He lives in Somerset West, Union of South Africa.